M000285722

Praise for *Facing an Exponential Future*

"*Facing an Exponential Future: Technology and the Community College* captivates the reader's mind and emotion with what seems an overwhelming plethora of change factors already shaping our world as we know it. Our individual challenge will be keeping up with the breadth and depth of such exponential change!"

—**Gary L. Rhodes**, president, J. Sargeant Reynolds
Community College, Richmond, Virginia

"Our nation was built on a blue collar, technical workforce, and our ability to refocus the education system to integrate and train a workforce for emerging technologies is critical for future growth of the economy! This book chronicles many of the current challenges."

—**Stan Shoun**, president, Ranken Technical
College, St. Louis, Missouri

"Darrel W. Staat presents an interesting read and certainly makes one step back and think how things have changed and the acceleration for the present and future."

—**Dr. Keith Miller**, president, Greenville Technical
College, Greenville, South Carolina

"This is a must-read for all community college administrators who want to continue to be a dominant force in workforce development in the twenty-first century. This book makes a compelling case that our current delivery models are antiquated, doomed, and that exploding technologies cannot be ignored. Furthermore, Staat and the contributors make the case in a forthright, understandable, and yet, entertaining way."

—**Theresa Gibson**, director of graduate education, Wingate University Ballantyne, Charlotte, North Carolina

"*Facing an Exponential Future: Technology and the Community College* punctuates the fact that leaders possessing innovation, creativity, and critical thinking skills are those best equipped to be successful in moving their institutions forward. The ability to embrace emerging technologies and apply them to better serve students and communities is a key requirement for today's effective leadership."

—**John Rainone**, president, Dabney S. Lancaster Community College, Clifton Forge, Virginia.

Facing an Exponential Future

Facing an Exponential Future

Technology and the Community College

Edited by
Darrel W. Staat

ROWMAN & LITTLEFIELD
Lanham • Boulder • New York • London

Published by Rowman & Littlefield
A wholly owned subsidiary of The Rowman & Littlefield Publishing Group, Inc.
4501 Forbes Boulevard, Suite 200, Lanham, Maryland 20706
www.rowman.com

Unit A, Whitacre Mews, 26-34 Stannary Street, London SE11 4AB

Copyright © 2018 by Darrel W. Staat

All rights reserved. No part of this book may be reproduced in any form or by any electronic or mechanical means, including information storage and retrieval systems, without written permission from the publisher, except by a reviewer who may quote passages in a review.

British Library Cataloguing in Publication Information Available

Library of Congress Cataloging-in-Publication Data

ISBN 978-1-4758-4361-3 (cloth: alk. paper)
ISBN 978-1-4758-4362-0 (pbk: alk. paper)
ISBN 978-1-4758-4363-7 (electronic)

♾ ™ The paper used in this publication meets the minimum requirements of American National Standard for Information Sciences—Permanence of Paper for Printed Library Materials, ANSI/NISO Z39.48-1992.

Printed in the United States of America

Contents

Preface   ix

Acknowledgments   xiii

Introduction   xv

1   Artificial Intelligence   1
        Eva Baucom and Natalie Winfree

2   Personal Robots   19
        Travis Gleaton, William "Ben" Shirley, and Carolyn Walker

3   3D Printing   33
        Shakitha Barner, Takeem L. Dean, and Carlos McCormick

4   Autonomous Vehicles and Drones   43
        Charlotte Blackwell, Amy Davis, and Cristy Holmes

5   The Internet of Things   57
        Darrel W. Staat

6   Genome Development: Medical   65
        Melodie Hunnicutt, Renie Johnston, and John "Scott" Stauble Jr.

7   Genome Development: Agricultural   77
        Melodie Hunnicutt, Renie Johnston, and John "Scott" Stauble Jr.

8   Nanotechnology   85
        Anthony Dozier, Lonnie F. Griffin III, and Jaime McLeod

9   Bitcoin and Blockchain   99
        Darrel W. Staat

10 Quantum Computing   103
      Darrel W. Staat

11 Exponential Leadership   109
      Darrel W. Staat

Appendix   115

About the Contributors   117

About the Editor   121

Preface

"You can actually hear the changes before you see some of them. Just
listen to how people speak these days. . . . Just a few years ago . . . but
then something changed. . . . Wow, I've never seen that before. . . . Well,
usually, but now I don't know anymore. . . ."

—Thomas Friedman

"The Community College in the 21st Century" is a course in The Community
College Executive Leadership EdD program at Wingate University Ballantyne in Charlotte, North Carolina. The goal of this course is to help future
community college leaders understand how to deal with changes that might
affect their institutions in the future.

Initially, to deal with that topic I read *The Fourth Industrial Revolution* by
Klaus Schwab, *The Industries of the Future* by Alec Ross, and *Rise of the
Robots* by Martin Ford hoping those books might give me insight into the
directions the future workforce was heading. They did. I fell into a rabbit hole.

I started down a forest path which led to Artificial Intelligence (AI), Artificial General Intelligence (AGI) and Artificial Super Intelligence (ASI), Deep
Blue, Watson, and the Singularity. I ran down another path leading toward
robots, those for manufacturing and those for personal use. I pushed back the
underbrush to find 3D printing producing everything from little objects to car
bodies and complete houses.

I scrambled across a meadow into genome developments and learned
how Watson was being used to assist in the medical and agricultural fields
and, beyond that, where understanding and manipulating the genome had
potential to improve health and well-being as we know it. I continued on to

nanotechnology where almost anything could be made by directing atoms and molecules.

I took another pathway leading to The Internet of Things (IoT) where everything was connected to everything else and they communicated with each other. Nearby I found a paved road leading to autonomous vehicles: self-driving cars and trucks, I peered down a tunnel into Bitcoin and Blockchain financing. I turned a corner, entered into the world of Quantum Computing with computing speeds that seemed to put Moore's Law into reverse gear.

What I found in my wanderings were as incompatible with my life experiences as Alice's journey through Wonderland. Her Mad Hatter was like 3D printing; her "off with her head" Queen was our Moore's Law; her Tweedledee and Tweedledum compared to the Internet of Things; her getting larger and smaller was quantum computing; her Cheshire Cat reminded me of genome possibilities; and our autonomous car was her ever-moving March Hare.

In my wanderings in the rabbit hole, I repeatedly came across the term exponential and found that understanding this word was critical to everything discussed in this book. To best understand what exponential means, here is a question.

Asked to make a choice between receiving $100,000 per day for an entire month or receiving a penny on the first day of the month and having it double every day of the month, which would you choose? (Ulrich, 2008).

The $100,000 a day for 30 days totals up a lot of money, some $3.0 million by the end of the month. How could a penny on day one of the month that doubled each day beat that? When the math is worked out, the penny-doubling each day for 30 days totaled $5.3 million. If only two more days were added, the $100,000 per day would total $3.2 million while the penny-doubling increased to $21.4 million. How does one explain that difference?

The $100,000 per day is a linear method of determining the total. The penny-doubling per day is an exponential method of developing the total. Metaphorically, the doubling process looks like a hockey stick. The doubling hardly changes as much of the month goes by traveling along the edge of the blade, but in the last few days of the month the total shoot ups like the shaft of the hockey stick.

Using Moore's Law, which projects a doubling in computer technology every eighteen months since about 1957 when it started with one transistor on a chip, the number had increased by the early 1970s to some 2,300 transistors on a chip. In 2018 there will be the power of 30 billion transistors on a chip (Neild, 2017). Exponential increase has become a reality.

Exponential increases in transistors per chip explain why there were only bag phones with limited telephone capabilities in the early 1990s, iPhones with a built-in camera and computer in the mid-2000s, and iPhone X in 2017 with immense technological capabilities. It also explains why Deep Blue, a computer, could beat Garry Kasparov, the best chess player in the world in 1997 and why Watson, another computer, could beat the world's best Jeopardy! players in 2010.

Exponential is a term that will help explain the why phenomenal technological changes are coming in the very near future. Every chapter in this book describes something that is changing in an exponential manner. If one is not aware of them and how they are going to affect the community college, it is because all of them are still in the early days of the penny-doubling, linear part of the month, seemingly not making much progress.

They are still on the metaphorical blade of the hockey stick, seeming to develop linearly. But as time goes by, the technologies discussed will suddenly move up the shaft of the hockey stick at breaknet speed.

And, if the current exponential speed of Moore's Law, doubling computer power every eighteen months, is not enough to consider, in the shadows is quantum computing, which uses atoms with double "ones" and "zeros." When fully developed, quantum computing will make Moore's Law look as if it was moving in reverse. Compare the speed of a mule pulling a plow in a field to a rocket heading to the moon . . . and maybe that comparison is much too slow.

It is hoped that this book can be of assistance to community college leaders, faculty, staff, board members, and students by making them aware of some of the exponential digital possibilities that technology will make available to human beings in the United States and around the world in the coming years and decades.

Becoming aware and understanding them is the first step, which will allow one to climb out of the rabbit hole. The second step is knowing they have to be dealt with. The third step is working to make them part of the community college environment. Time is of the essence; community college leaders need to start today.

Since my work at Wingate University is to prepare graduate students to become successful community college leaders, I asked them to jump into the rabbit hole with me, explore on multiple fronts, and research what might affect the community college world. Seven of the chapters in this book are the result of their work. Our combined efforts present the research results, suggest changes community colleges may have to deal with in the future, and estimate when those changes most likely will arrive.

REFERENCES

Neild, David. (2017, June 6). IBM's new computer can fit 30 billion transistors on your fingertip. *Science Alert.* https://www.sciencealert.com/new-computer-can-fit-30-billion-transistors-on-your-fingertip.

Uldrich, Jack. (2007). *Jump the Curve.* Avon, MA: Adams Media.

Acknowledgments

To begin with, I would like to thank my loving wife, Beverly, who put up with my endless hours in the office reading, writing, and what seemed to her, the purchasing of a never-ending number of books. She encouraged and supported me without question.

Next, I would like to thank the students of Cohort 4 in the EdD Community College Executive Leadership Program at Wingate University in Charlotte, North Carolina, who, in groups, researched and wrote seven of the chapters in this book. Their excitement and enthusiasm for the task is greatly appreciated. Their names are included with the chapters they wrote and in the About the Contributors section.

In addition, I am thankful for the support of my colleague and longtime friend, Dr. John McKay. He continually brought me articles that were of interest to the development of this book. His support for this task was solid throughout.

Others I greatly appreciate include Dr. Annette Digby, dean of the Thayer School of Education at Wingate University, who upon hearing of my interest in developing this book gave me support and encouragement. Also Ms. Theresa Gibson, director of Graduate Education at Wingate University, whose leadership and goal-oriented behavior set an example of excellence for all of us.

A special thanks to my daughter, Laura Staat, who painstakingly typed up the final draft of the book for submission to the publisher and provided a design for the cover of the book.

Introduction

"Being able to anticipate the future instead of reacting to what's happening now is going to be key to survival."

—Brigette Hyacinth

In the middle of the twenty-first century, the community college is heading toward a series of technologies that will directly affect the administration, faculty, staff, students, the business community, local economic development agencies, and perhaps, the institution's very existence. These technologies, which appear with little warning, will impact community colleges with a series of continuous, rapid-fire, culture-changing events.

If community college leaders, faculty, staff, and board members are caught off guard as to what they will face, their service to students, the business community and local economic development could be headed for disaster. The goal of this book is to assist those leading, teaching, and learning in community colleges to understand the changes in the offing that will affect them and suggest how they might deal with them.

Today, the following technologies are developing at an exponential velocity: Artificial Intelligence, Personal Robots, 3D Printing, Autonomous Vehicles, The Internet of Things, Genome Developments, Nanotechnology, Bitcoin and Blockchain, and Quantum Computing. They will affect the community college causing transformations in offerings, day-to-day operations, and the continuous retraining of faculty, staff, and administration.

The community college of 2050 will not resemble the institution of 2018. The technologies listed above will in a mere thirty-two years transform it phenomenally. It would be helpful if the technologies appeared on the scene one at a time, with sufficient time between each to catch one's breath and get used to what is happening. But, that is not the case.

The thirty-two-year time period promises to be chaotic, and difficult to understand. It is racing into the heart of the community colleges far faster than anything seen before, and with a transforming power not experienced previously. For community colleges to remain viable and successful for its constituents will demand the skills of a tightrope walker combined with the ability of the commander guiding a rocket to the moon.

The technologies will not slow down; they will not give quarter. When their development metaphorically hits the shaft of the hockey stick and sky-rockets upward, dealing with them will seem impossible to those unaware or ignorant. Although each technology will create its own issues, the combination of them, at much the same time, will demand leaders, faculty, and staff who are well prepared.

This book discusses the beginning of a very fast race that is in the starting blocks. The vision of the future it presents may be frightening and difficult to understand. On the other hand, the race provides an opportunity for leaders, faculty, and staff to begin comprehending what is coming and search for a secure place in the transforming, technology-driven world of the future.

This book describes the technologies, discusses the impact on the community college environment, and provides recommendations for modifying college operations. It is hoped that the information provided will be of assistance to those involved in the community college movement.

Chapter 1

Artificial Intelligence

Eva Baucom and Natalie Winfree

"Intellectuals solve problems. Geniuses prevent them."

—Albert Einstein

There are varying opinions regarding artificial intelligence (AI) and its impact on education and the workforce; some view AI as a pro and others see it as a con. No matter one's opinion on AI, one thing is for certain, the workforce will look vastly different in years to come.

The type of education needed to enter today's workforce is already changing, but what is anticipated to be needed in the future will morph into new systems, processes, and ways of working. It is important that community colleges stay abreast of the changing needs and learn to develop programs equipped to train the workers of the future.

ARTIFICIAL INTELLIGENCE HISTORY
AND SITUATION TODAY

There may be as many as eight or more different definitions of artificial intelligence in existence today. The one most commonly used defines AI as "the theory and development of computer systems able to perform tasks that normally require human intelligence" (Schatsky, Muraskin, and Gurumurthy, 2014, p. 3).

This term provides a broad definition of what artificial intelligence is; however, breaking AI down even further encompasses many areas which include: machine learning, natural language processing, expert systems, vision, speech, planning, and robotics (Buscemi, 2017). While most people may not understand what these areas are, they are already familiar with AI and have incorporated it into their lives using assistance from a personal robot such as Siri, Alexa, or Amazon Echo.

Many have invested in an iRobot Roomba vacuum system, most have heard the term autonomous vehicle, and who could forget IBM's Watson? Essentially, AI is used to "streamline [business] processes and make complex decisions faster" (Mahidhar and Schatsky, 2013, p. 2). For businesses this provides significant cost savings and efficiency.

AI has already infiltrated many aspects of common human activities by automating many everyday processes. Netflix provides users with a list of suggested movies based on their previous choices. Amazon and other online retailers provide similar suggestions to shoppers. "Automakers are using computer vision and other cognitive technologies to enhance their products" making vehicles safer (Schatsky, Muraskin, and Gurumurthy, 2015, p. 117)

Cell phones use voice recognition for dictating text messages. Customer service lines use automation to sort through incoming phone calls. Humans obtain money through ATM withdrawals without ever setting foot in banks. Computer programs are being used to write news reports and sports stories.

However, the term artificial intelligence did not make its mark in history until the 1956 month-long conference at Dartmouth College in Hanover, New Hampshire, when John McCarthy conceived the term as a way to describe topics well advanced for the time (Lewis, 2014). Since then, AI has had moments of progression and years of setbacks. Research on AI was renewed in 1996 after IBM's chess-playing computer known as Deep Blue defeated Garry Kasparov, who up until that time had been the world champion (Bundy, 2017)

IBM's Watson was conceptualized in 2004, the labor intensive project began in 2007, and in February 2011, Watson successfully "beat the World champions at the '*Jeopardy!*' general-knowledge quiz game" (Bundy, 2017, p. 41). Following this win, Watson's capabilities have moved into other sectors such as "healthcare, finance, entertainment, and retail" (Gaudin, 2016, para. 2)

Machine Learning and Moore's Law

One popular AI term is Moore's Law. Named after Intel cofounder Gordon Moore, who in 1956 observed and predicted "that computing would dramatically increase in power, and decrease in relative cost, at an exponential pace" (Intel, 2017) has been proven true. Computer storage has doubled every eighteen months and the costs have dramatically decreased over the years. The ability of today's iPhone has significantly improved from the original bag phone to where it is essentially a combination of phone and computer in a compact device for much less cost than the original bag phone.

A second well-known AI term is machine learning. Not only is the increase in computer power significant, but machine learning means even more increases in automation. Machine learning is the "ability of computer systems to improve their performance by exposure to data without the need to follow explicitly programmed instructions" (Schatsky et al., 2014, p. 6).

Both Moore's Law and machine learning can be seen in IBM's Watson. IBM was able to double the precision of Watson's answers in a few years leading up to its famous *Jeopardy!* victory in 2011 by programming it to learn on its own (Buscemi, 2017).

As long as machines have access to data in order to perform a specific task, they can learn for themselves (Buscemi, 2017). This information is then used to make predictions. These predictions are used by companies to "Generate insights that can help reduce costs, improve efficiency, increase revenues, improve effectiveness, and enhance customer service" (Schatsky et al., 2015, p. 121).

Intelligent Automation

The workforce continues to rely upon and expand its intelligent automation. Mahidhar and Schatsky (2013) define intelligent automation as "the combination of artificial intelligence and automation (p. 1). These systems "sense and synthesize vast amounts of information and can automate entire processes or workflows, learning and adapting as they go" (p. 1).

It is these intelligent automation systems that are infiltrating "nearly every sector of the economy" (p. 3) from housework to vehicles, from medical diagnoses and treatments to manufacturing, and every market in between. These systems are used in collaboration with humans as a way to "streamline processes and make complex decisions faster" (p. 2). Intelligent automation, another term for machine learning is being used around the world watching for threats of violence, monitoring credit-risk information, and making decisions about patient care.

The continued rise of intelligent automation will change the skills needed for employment, the types of jobs available, and create the need for additional risk management. As of 2014, Schatsky and Muraskin expected cognitive technologies to grow tremendously during the following five years especially because of a push to commercialize them. It has been predicted that "by 2020, automation and robots will eliminate roughly 5 million jobs in 15 of the world's developed and emerging economies" (Engelking, 2017, p. 38–39).

Progress and Limitations

"Machines have always automated tasks that previously required human effort and attention . . . usually by employing very different techniques"

(Kaplan, 2017, p. 37). One example is the move from typewriters to computers. Typical office settings in the 1950s and 1960s required a secretary or typist who would type memos and letters and then retype them in their entirety for editing purposes or when amendments were required. This also required maintaining physical files and increased wait time between creating a memo and sending it out.

Fast forward to the twenty-first century where all offices rely on computers for creating, saving, and sending memos and letters, not to mention using computers to create presentations, spreadsheets, and share data, all with a touch of a button eliminating the need for an assistant. While computers and other technologies are used in everyday activities, they still pose limitations. This is because "machines don't have minds" (p. 37); they "cannot think" (Schatsky, Muraskin, and Gurumurthy, 2015, p. 115).

Unlike humans who possess "general intelligence" (Engelking, 2017, p. 34) where they have the ability to easily change tasks and perform varying tasks, AI systems are "narrow in scope" (Bundy, 2017, p. 40). In other words, AI systems are "fantastic at single, well-defined tasks" (Engelking, 2017, p. 34), but, for anything outside of that task, they are "incredibly dumb" (Bundy, 2017, p. 42).

Deep Blue was designed to play chess, but could not physically move the pieces. Even IBM's Watson, which is utilized across different disciplines, is narrow in scope. While for now, it is the most advanced "cognitive computing vision" (Dubhashi and Lappin, 2017, p. 45) technology in existence, the Watson used to diagnose and treat cancer will have a focus vastly different from the Watson used to draft Toronto Raptors players.

These differences stem from the algorithms that make up the AI system. "AI generally seeks to solve particular tasks" (Dubhashi and Lappin, 2017, p. 44); therefore humans must choose what to include in the data sets and adjust the parameters accordingly.

Impact on the Global Economy

From a business perspective, areas such as US manufacturing will become "more competitive with low-wage countries" (Ford, 2015, p. 9) due to cost savings from the elimination of human workers. While machines create cost savings and faster, more efficient production, the biggest problem is "machines do not consume" (Ford, 2015, p. 196).

It is the human workers who earn wages and spend those wages, which perpetuates the economy. If machines are replacing human workers, then there is no discretionary income to spend and the economy will suffer. And if no one can afford to buy what the machine is producing, then both the human and the machine will be out of work.

Even more worrisome is the fact that machines, automation, and AI are not just taking over the low-wage or bad jobs, but are threatening higher-skill jobs as well. The traditional answer to job displacement is more education and better skills; however, if automation eliminates higher-skill jobs, then education and better skills are not necessarily going to eliminate unemployment.

One answer across the research is that humans must learn to work and collaborate with the machines. But, before higher education leaders can determine what programs and training will be needed for the future workforce, they must understand how technology is progressing and in the short, mid, and long term.

PREDICTED CHANGES IN ARTIFICIAL INTELLIGENCE

Artificial intelligence is predicted to accelerate at a rapid pace, which promises both small and significant changes in their personal and professional lives of Americans.

Short Term

This narrow scope should not dismiss the fact that "AI has massive potential" (Kenny, 2017, p. 1). Dubhashi and Lappin (2017) confirm that a "human doctor aided by a Watson cognitive assistant would be more effective in diagnosing and treating diseases than either Watson or the doctor working separately" (p. 45).

Treatment centers like the Memorial Sloan-Kettering Cancer Center in New York City are already utilizing IBM Watson for this very reason. Watson has the ability to process large volumes of data quickly, evaluate cases and treatment prognosis, and help the oncology team determine the best, most up-to-date individualized treatment plan based on each patient (Memorial Sloan-Kettering Cancer Center, 2017). A human worker would not have the time or resources to perform these same tasks as quickly or as efficiently.

Mid Term

Per Kaplan (2017), "the labor market constantly evolves in response to automation" (p. 37) and he points out that it is not the jobs that become automated; it is the tasks. So, with this reasoning, the nature of the tasks the worker performs will determine if that worker will be replaced or made more productive.

In simpler terms, if a worker performs "repetitive or well-defined procedures" with "a clear-cut goal, then their . . . employment is at risk" (p. 37). Other research agrees, "AI technologies could displace low-wage, uneducated workers" (Engelking, 2017, p. 39). In fact, workers are already being displaced by advances in technology.

Online retailers such as Amazon and eBay are providing a "competitive advantage" (Ford, 2015, p. 16) over the traditional "brick and mortar stores" (p. 16) where customers can shop from the comfort of their home or office at all hours of the day and night and still enjoy "immediate gratification after a purchase" (p. 16) through the advantage of same day or next day delivery.

With the convenience of online shopping, more brick and mortar stores will be closing their doors thus laying off low-wage workers. And, for those stores that remain open, they will look for ways to automate their processes from self-checkout aisles to robots that restock shelves. In addition, shoppers will rely "on their phones as a way to shop, pay, and get help and information about products while in traditional retail settings" (p. 19–20) eliminating the need for retail workers further.

Similar situations can be expected with service jobs such as in the fast-food industry. With the rise in how much minimum wage workers earn, restaurant owners are seeking ways to lower costs and increase efficiency. This can change how fast food is ordered, prepared, and delivered. Kiosks or touch panel screens will be used to order and pay for food eliminating any human interaction.

In addition, with more and more people relying on their cell phones to shop, they will then have the ability to place their order and pay for items ahead of time at the fast-food restaurant of their choice using their cell phone. They will be able to pick up their order at the drive-thru; thus, eliminating much of the typical human interaction and wait times and making fast food even faster with fewer human workers necessary.

Long Term

The long-term future of AI is a topic of debate among experts. Currently, narrow AI is common in contemporary life and is viewed as a supplemental tool to humans. This type of AI has a specific purpose as designated by the human controller. Some experts, however, predict that within the next century, narrow AI will morph into artificial general intelligence (AGI) or superintelligence (ASI) (Baer, 2015).

The Artificial General Intelligence Society (2014) defines AGI as "general-purpose systems with intelligence comparable to that of the human mind (and perhaps ultimately well beyond human general intelligence)" (AGI Society).

In theory, AGI will be able to achieve any cognitive or emotional act as a human without human intervention.

With the "exponential growth in the power of computer chips" (Dubhashi and Lappin, 2017, p. 43) as dictated by Moore's Law, AI will continue to expand, potentially surpassing human capabilities and eventually leading to what is called the Singularity. Add soon-to-be on the scene Quantum computing and the Singularity will be given an extremely rapid boost beyond Moore's Law.

The Singularity. One idea that neither proponents nor opponents of AI can agree on is the idea of a "technological singularity" (Walsh, 2016, "Introduction" section). Dubhashi and Lappin (2017) describe the Singularity as a point when machines "correct their own defects and program themselves to produce artificial superintelligent agents that far surpass human capabilities in virtually every cognitive domain" (p. 43).

Many experts predict the Singularity as the time when the human race ceases to exist. Ray Kurzweil, Google's director of engineering, predicted that the technological singularity will happen within the next thirty years (as cited by Galeon and Reedy, 2017). In a recent interview with *Futurism*, Kurzweil stated, "I have set the date 2045 for the 'Singularity' which is when we will multiply our effective intelligence a billion fold by merging with the intelligence we have created" (as cited by Galeon and Reedy, "Kurzweil Claims . . .", 2017).

Not all experts agree that the Singularity will happen. Walsh (2016) argues that intelligence depends on many things other than simply thinking faster. Instead, intelligence is also contributed to "many years of experience and training" that machines do not have or can replicate (Walsh, 2016, "The 'Fast Thinking Dog' Argument" section).

Regardless, the topic of the technological singularity conjures up much debate from experts within the AI community. It is not just a science fiction notion but has, under the right conditions, a real chance of becoming a reality, which is a very frightening possibility.

THE IMPACT OF AI ON THE COMMUNITY COLLEGE

The community college is at the forefront when the workforce becomes displaced. And while "new technologies can destroy some jobs, they also create new jobs that absorb the displaced workforce" (Dubhaski and Lappin, 2017, p. 45). It is up to the community college to be ready to retrain these displaced workers and educate the future workforce.

No longer will the community college be able to rely on already established programs but will need to develop programs where people partner with machines and learn skills necessary to remain competitive. This combination of "humans and machines is more powerful than either one of them alone" (p. 45) at least for the time being. This seemingly strange combination will be facing the workforce in the near future.

Kenny (2017) believes "the right approach is to focus on training workers in the right skills" (p. 2) but what are those right skills? For the professions that rely on social skills, such as personal shopper, performer, and advisor, they may be the least impacted by AI. However, many of the skills needed for the future workforce will require vocational training in areas of information technology, cybersecurity, and cloud infrastructure engineering.

With the fast growth of AI, there may be career fields created that have not yet been thought of. This may lead to new and innovative curriculum programs at the community college level. But changes affecting community colleges will be seen in the short term, mid term, and long term.

Short Term

The short-term effects are those in the immediate future. AI is already changing the workforce; therefore, over the next three to five years, community colleges will need to embrace workforce development programs that provide training consistent with the impending information technology enhancements and be prepared with programs to the resulting displaced workers.

As automation takes over the routine jobs and businesses fight to be cutting-edge, human workers will need the skills to keep up with the high tech demands. But, before these displaced workers can succeed in high tech programs, they may need to build their basic education skills.

Since many of the immediately displaced workers are expected to come from the retail, the fast-food industry, truck driving, and customer service where high education is not required, community colleges should anticipate a surge in enrollment in the basic skills classes and remedial courses.

Enhancing their basic skills will be necessary before enrolling these displaced workers into a high tech curriculum program. Further, because many of these displaced workers are accustomed to earning an income, community colleges would benefit from providing job-ready certificate programs for a quicker turnaround time back into the workforce.

Mid Term

As this technological trend suggests, the community college must recognize the need to update programs and create new programs that align with the high tech needs of businesses. It is during this mid-term that the jobs "will involve collaborating with the machines" (Ford, 2015, p. 122).

With the impact of Moore's Law on technology, programs will need to be consistently updated in order to properly prepare students for a competitive workforce targeting electrical and electronic skills. However, this could emerge as a "small population of elite workers" (Ford, 2015, p. 123) unless the community college and businesses can collaborate and determine true workforce needs and innovative career options.

In an attempt to deal with the increasing technology, community colleges will need to incorporate AI across the curriculum exposing all students as a way to familiarize them with it. For those displaced workers who are least familiar with technology, much like the need for remedial classes, they may need to enroll in a type of remedial or introductory AI class designed to expose and enhance computer skills and knowledge for the twenty-first century.

As more workers are displaced by automation and new high tech businesses are formed, community colleges will need to adapt to increases in enrollment and be prepared to meet students where they are in terms of skills and background. Career counseling will become a focal point in order to match a person's abilities and skill level to a suitable career pathway.

It is likely that colleges will not only introduce new program offerings, but they will introduce varying ways for students to obtain certifications and degrees as a way to remain competitive. Community colleges will have to compete with a growing trend that includes massive open online courses (MOOCs) where students can sign up for an internet-based class for free or for very low cost and within weeks receive a certificate of completion.

According to Ford (2015), MOOCs "compete for the same people who might otherwise enroll in more traditional classes" and "are most likely to attract students who are already highly motivated to seek further education" (p. 135). In the battle for quality education at the lowest price, it is likely that community colleges might lose out to MOOCs.

Therefore, community colleges may seek ways to provide quality education at a cost savings to the students. One way is to rely on algorithms and machine grading as a "laborsaving" (Ford, 2015, p. 129) strategy and utilize one instructor to teach hundreds of students at a time, which would be a significant change for community colleges.

Long Term

AI could lead to negative results for the community college over the long term. While the initial expectation is an increase in enrollment, with an increase in competition from four year colleges and universities and Ivy League schools offering MOOCs, community colleges could experience a tremendous decline in enrollment following that initial influx.

As new educational technologies emerge, the need for faculty and staff will decline further. As of 2015, adaptive learning systems were already being incorporated and their effects studied. These systems "follow the progress of individual students," "offer personalized instruction and assistance," "adjust the pace of learning to match" the student, and "provide what amounts to a robotic tutor" (Ford, 2015, p. 143), thus eliminating the need for the human worker.

Worst-case scenario, if community colleges do not take action, they could become obsolete. Best case, if community colleges continually stay abreast of the changes in technology, they could become a valuable segment of hands-on education in the future.

FUTURE PROGRAMS AT COMMUNITY COLLEGES

Community colleges in the twenty-first century must be adaptive to the changing landscape and leaders must be calculated risk takers in order to provide innovative programs for students, business partners, local economic development agencies, and the community in general. Before adding any programs, community college leaders should examine labor market data, for partnerships with businesses and industries, and consider the feasibility of programs to add.

AI presents exceptional opportunities for community colleges to transform current programs and add new programs. Community colleges should consider adding AI-related programs in the short, mid, and long term to position for current and future success and sustainability.

Short Term

Narrow AI has already infiltrated everyday personal and professional life, and this trend is only predicted to grow. The White House Artificial Intelligence Economy Report (2016) summarizes that "AI changes the nature of work and the skills demanded by the labor market" and significant investments in education and training are needed to "ensure that Americans have access to affordable post-secondary education" ("Strategy #2: Educate . . ." section).

Community colleges are in the best position to be the premier training center for AI programs. Some programs focusing on 3D printing, robotics, drones, and megatronics already exist in community colleges across the United States, and these programs lay the foundation for additional AI programs. The next three to five years present a multitude of opportunities for community colleges to offer curriculum programs, certificates, and short-term customized training to train workers for the twenty-first century.

The US Department of Labor (Kishore, 2017) predicts a 16 percent increase in industrial machinery mechanics and machinery maintenance workers by 2024. Community colleges should continue to offer machining programs in order to meet this workforce demand.

It is imperative, however, that community colleges work with business and industry leaders in AI to ensure the machining training is reflective of the changing machines and technology. Community colleges should create partnerships with businesses that utilize AI in machining to implement customized short- and long-term training that upskills incumbent workers.

In addition to revamping current programs in machining, community colleges should also consider adding programs in AI engineering. An AI engineer may work with large data sets involved with machine learning and predictive analytics. According to Lynch (2016), "Machine Learning Engineer is the single most popular title for AI-related jobs" ("The Most Popular Job Title . . ." section). Jobs in machine learning engineering include "natural language processing, computer vision, and predictions/insights/recommendations" (Lynch, 2016, "The Most Popular Job Title . . ." section).

Cybersecurity is another area of AI that is expected to grow tremendously. The US Department of Labor (2015) anticipates Information Security Analysts jobs to increase "much faster than average" at a rate of 18 percent by 2024. Stark (2016) believes there is a looming "severe cyber-security labor shortage, expected to reach 1.5 million job openings by 2019" ("There Simply Are Not Enough . . ." section).

Currently, information security analysts typically require a bachelor's degree for an entry-level position. Some community colleges have already implemented a cybersecurity training certificate and Applied Associates in Science degree; however, the labor market will demand more workers in this area.

Mid Term

In the next five to ten years, virtually every job will transition to using AI in some capacity. As a result, community colleges should prepare for an influx of workers seeking industry-specific upskilling and retraining. Industries expected to be impacted the most by artificial intelligence include healthcare, finance, security, and retail (Buscemi, 2017).

Training within these areas includes integrating AI with existing technology, training employees how to use AI, interpreting results, and maintenance (Buscemi, 2017). Partnerships with businesses and industries will be more important than ever to ensure community colleges offer relevant and innovative training to meet workforce demands in a changing technological landscape.

Long Term

The next ten years and beyond bring much uncertainty and speculation about the role of AI in both society and community college programs. Some question whether machines will completely take over education and training;

others are concerned that brick and mortar postsecondary education will even still exist.

In order to remain competitive and relevant to students and businesses, community colleges must look beyond ten years and predict the AI programs of the future. Colleges must be more flexible and adapting than ever before as AI promises to transform program offerings.

Kurzweil predicts AGI to emerge as early as 2029 (Galeon and Reedy, 2017). Over the next ten years, jobs will emerge to aid in the transition from narrow AI to AGI. In order to make this transition, robots will need extensive development in emotions and empathy. Wilson, Daugherty, and Moreni-Bianzino (2017) consider this type of job to be an "empathy trainer" ("Trainer" section) or individuals who develop AI systems to show and understand compassion.

Specific training areas within empathy training include customer-language tone and meaning, smart-machine interactions, and worldview perspective (Wilson et al., 2017). Community colleges should consider creating a robot empathy training program to address the future needs in this area. Businesses will also need more trainers and sustainers to integrate artificial intelligence technology into existing software and processes (Wilson et al., 2017).

Public safety will continue to remain a concern as machines transform from narrow AI to AGI. If robots ever reach the capacity to overtake humans, then public safety and human survival will become the number one priority for the country. Even if the singularity never happens, technology that allows individuals to beam personal holograms is already in existence and will likely only increase in frequency.

Frank (2017) stated, "Regulating the free movement of augmented reality and hologram technology will be an increasingly painful headache for police forces and city officials going forward" ("You Can Ban a Person . . ."). In order to address this possibility, community colleges should consider adding programs that specifically deal with public safety and machines, such as programs in law enforcement training for robots, which will require a completely different approach to safety than humans, and specific training will be necessary to provide safety officers with the necessary skills.

ADVICE FOR COMMUNITY COLLEGE LEADERS

Community college leaders face an exciting and unpredictable future. AI has the potential to completely transform college operations for delivery methods to program offerings and threatens the complete existence of physical college campuses. In order to champion the role of community colleges through this transformation, community college leaders must be flexible, adaptive, and forward-thinking.

Leaders must be bold and develop a "healthy obsession" with technology to estimate the pace at which technology is accelerating and shift the college direction accordingly (Solomon, 2017, "Survey the Landscape" section).

Short Term

In the short term, community college leaders should gather as much information about AI as possible. This includes reading journals, attending AI conferences, speaking with peers across the country, and forming partnerships with businesses and industries that work with AI. Community college leaders need to examine labor market predictions, study higher education institutions across the world, and remain informed on developments in an attempt to prepare the college for the impending transformation.

The AI field opens up many opportunities for community colleges to become the premier training resource in all postsecondary education. College leaders should form a regional AI coalition to discuss ideas, determine programming, and position the community college as a whole for future success.

Finally, community college leaders should identify the consequences of either embracing or not embracing AI (Solomon, 2017). Leaders must use data to make a compelling argument to all key stakeholders as to the role AI will play in current and future plans for the college.

Mid Term

Community college leaders must be prepared for this wave of new program implementation, rapid changes, and potential influx of workers. Colleges that are early adapters have the biggest potential for success in AI training, and such early adapters have the opportunity to create state, regional, and national models of training.

Over the next five to ten years, community college leaders should seek to find the AI niche most beneficial to their community. Leaders should consider what area of AI the college can be the best in the world at and develop a "hedgehog concept" around niche AI programs (Collins, 2001, p. 90).

Long Term

The worst-case scenario is that human community college leaders may not even be needed in the long term. If the singularity actually happens, then today's education in its totality may become superfluous. However, the more likely future presents a transformed college landscape and learning experience still primarily managed by humans and supplemented with artificial intelligence.

Community college leaders must find the correct balance in face-to-face interactions, machine-driven education, and program offerings that promote the mission of the college. Community college leaders must be comfortable with uncertainty, yet not comfortable with the status quo.

ADVICE FOR STUDENTS

AI is the mother of opportunity for students. Just as the internet opened up a whole new world of job and training opportunities in the 1990s and early 2000s, AI is poised to do the same for 2018 and beyond. AI also threatens to replace future jobs as well. Students should examine the short-, mid-, and long-term impact of AI on their education and training courses and career choice.

Short Term

The best advice for students in the short term is to take time and effort to research current and future labor market needs to determine what careers will be most relevant and the type of training necessary. Students may not have the knowledge or experience to do this independently and should seek out the help of a career counselor or advisor for guidance.

Students should also explore potential career options through internships, shadowing, or attending guest speaker presentations on campus. As AI has the potential to change the way colleges deliver instruction, students should examine how they learn best to determine if face-to-face or online instruction is most effective.

Mid Term

Often, students pursue the same career of a parent or family member. Students become familiar with that career and see firsthand the type of life-style that is awarded by it. In the mid term, however, AI may change the types of careers so drastically that students will not be able to seek the same careers as their parents and family members because they will no longer exist.

In order to gain exposure to new career options, students should attend career-focused camps in AI while in middle school and high school, take career assessments, and continue to seek out career counselors for assistance. Students should evaluate the value of a degree or certificate from a community college in comparison to a four-year bachelor's degree or no degree at all. Being knowledgeable will help students remain competitive in a rapidly changing environment.

Long Term

The long-term outlook for students promises major changes in education. The traditional education model is likely to look drastically different. For students, the only thing for certain in the long term is unpredictability.

The best advice for students during this time is to remain lifelong learners. Even though AI is accelerating rapidly, students have weathered major technology advances, such as the emergence of the cell phone and internet. The key to remaining relevant in the changing landscape of the future is to dedicate oneself to lifelong learning and seek retraining continuously.

CONCLUSION

AI presents many uncertainties, yet endless opportunities, for those willing to take significant calculated risks. Rapid advancements in the area promise to bring changes to both personal and professional lives, and those changes will certainly impact the American labor market.

Community colleges are in the best position to champion the training and education necessary to meet the transformed workforce demands and skills. Understanding the current situation with AI, however, is simply not enough. Community college leaders must be forward thinkers, innovators, and knowledge seekers in order to succeed and thrive in the short, mid, and long term.

REFERENCES

Artificial General Intelligence Society. (2014). AGI Society. http://www.agisociety.org.

Baer, D. (2015, December 18). 9 crazy things that could happen after the singularity: When robots become smarter than humans. *Business Insider.* http://www.businessinsider.com/predictions-for-after-singularity-2015-11.

Bundy, A. (2017). Smart machines are not a threat to humanity. *Communications of the ACM, 60*(2), 40–42. doi:10.1145/2950042.

Buscemi, P. (2017, April 23). A b2b marketer's guide to artificial intelligence. *Business2Community.* http://www.business2community.com/b2b-marketing/b2b-marketers-guide-artificial-intelligence-01828255#MeDVXmai4Ftp01Mq.97.

Collins, J. (2001). *Good to great: Why some companies make the leap...and others don't.* New York, NY: HarperCollins.

Dubhashi, D., & Lappin, S. (2017). AI dangers: Imagined and real. *Communications of the ACM, 60*(2), 43–45. doi:10.1145/2953876.

Engelking, C. (2017, April). Commonsense: A band of Seattle computer scientists is on a mission to make artificial intelligence actually intelligent. *Discover.* http://discovermagazine.com/2017/april-2017/cultivating-common-sense.

Ford. M. (2015). *Rise of the robots: Technology and the threat of a jobless future.* New York: Basic Books.

Frank, A. (2017, March 17). You can ban a person, but what about their hologram? *Singularity Hub*. https://singularityhub.com/2017/03/17/you-can-ban-a-person-but-what-about-their-hologram/.

Galeon, D., & Reedy, C. (2017, March 15). Kurzweil claims that the singularity will happen by 2045. https://futurism.com/kurzweil-claims-that-the-singularity-will-happen-by-2045/.

Gaudin, S. (2016, October 27). IBM: In 5 years, watson a.i. will be behind your every decision. *Computerworld*. http://www.computerworld.com/article/3135852/artificial-intelligence/ibm-in-5-years-watson-ai-will-be-behind-your-every-decision.html.

Intel. (2017, July 3). 50 years of Moore's law. *Intel*. https://www.intel.com/content/www/us/en/silicon-innovations/moores-law-technology.html.

Kaplan, J. (2017). Artificial intelligence: Think again. *Communications of the ACM, 60*(1), 36–38. doi:10.1145/2950039.

Kenny, D. (2017). Bill Gates is wrong: the solution to ai taking jobs is training, not taxes. *Wired*. https://www.wired.com/2017/04/bill-gates-wrong-solution-ai-taking-jobs-training-not-taxes/.

Kishore, S. (2017, April 3). Jobs in the age of artificial intelligence. https://chatbots-magazine.com/jobs-in-the-age-of-artificial-intelligence-e971c84b8de8.

Lewis, T. (2014, December). A brief history of artificial intelligence. *Live Science*. https://www.livescience.com/49007-history-of-artificial-intelligence.html.

Lynch, S. (2016, November 4). What are the artificial intelligence jobs? http://blog.udacity.com/2016/11/artificial-intelligence-jobs.html.

Mahidhar, V., & Schatsky, D. (2013). Intelligent automation: A new era of innovation. *Signals for Strategists*. Deloitte University Press.

Memorial Sloan Kettering Cancer Center. (July 2, 2017). About us. *Watson Oncology*. https://www.mskcc.org/about/innovative-collaborations/watson-Oncology.

Schatsky, D., Muraskin, C., & Gurumurthy, R. (2014). *Demystifying artificial intelligence: What business leaders need to know about cognitive technologies*. São Paulo, Brazil: Deloitte University Press.

Schatsky, D., Muraskin, C., & Gurumurthy, R. (2015). Cognitive technologies: The real opportunities for business. *Deloitte Review, 16*, 115–129. São Paulo, Brazil: Deloitte Toche Tohmatsu Limited: UK.

Solomon, L. K. (2017, July 12). Why every leader needs a healthy obsession with technology. *Singularity Hub*. https://singularityhub.com/2017/07/12.

Stark, J. R. (2016, September 27). There are simply not enough cyber-security specialists. *Compliance Week*. https://www.complianceweek.com/blogs/john-reed-stark/there-simply-are-not-enough-cyber-security-specialists#.WWefAYTyu00.

United States Department of Labor. (2015). Occupational outlook handbook: Information security analysts. https://www.bls.gov/ooh/computer-and-information-technology/information-security-analysts.htm.

Walsh, T. (2016). The singularity may never be near. https://arxiv.org/pdf/1602.06462.pdf.

White House. (2016). White House artificial intelligence economy report. https://www.whitehouse.gov/sites/whitehouse.gov/files/images/EMBARGOED%20AI%20Economy%20Report.pdf.

Wilson, H. J., Daugherty, P. R., & Morini-Bianzino, N. (2017). The jobs that artificial intelligence will create. *MIT Sloan Management Review.* http://sloanreview.mit.edu/article/will-ai-create-as-many-jobs-as-it-eliminates/.

Chapter 2

Personal Robots

Travis Gleaton, William "Ben" Shirley, and Carolyn Walker

"Technology is not kind. It does not wait. It does not say please. It slams into existing systems and often destroys them . . . while creating a new one."

—Joseph Schumpeter

The robotic revolution is transforming society from where people work to how people care for the elderly to the intimate relationships people establish (Lin, 2012). A major impact is the creation of personal robots. No longer will robots be found only in industrial areas, but they will be located in the home and institutional settings (Dahl and Boulos, 2013; Knight, 2015).

For example, Kharpal (2015) found that one in ten households will have some form of a home or personal robot by 2020. As personal robots become more ubiquitous, they will have a major impact on education institutions. To understand this transformation the following analysis provides an overview of personal robots, how personal robots will change over the next twenty years, and how community colleges will be impacted.

CURRENT STATUS OF PERSONAL SERVICE ROBOTS

The Rise of Personal Robots

Historically industrial robots have been designed to perform what researcher Patrick Lin called "the three Ds . . . jobs that are dull, dirty, or dangerous" (Lin, 2012, p. 4). Originally, these robots were designed for the manufacturing sector to complete monotonous and dangerous jobs (Lin, 2012).

Industrial robots eventually transformed economies by affecting employment opportunities. Industrial robots are what Ford (2015) called a disruptive technology, one that "has the power to devastate entire industries and upend specific sectors of the economy and job market" (Ford, 2015, p. xvii). In the manufacturing sector many individuals experienced some form of disruption caused by robotic technology and automation, resulting in people losing their jobs (Ford, 2015).

Since the beginning of the twenty-first century, robots have been designed for personal use to assist people in a variety of tasks, such as healthcare, education, life coach, therapy, and in their home life (Dahl and Boulos, 2013; Knight, 2015). The tasks personal service robots perform include, but are not limited to, cleaning, multimedia assistance, home security, rehabilitation, educational services, and companionship (IFR, 2016).

Moreover, personal service robots vary based on need and function, (Hegel, Muhl, Wrede, Hielscher-Fastabend, and Sagerer, 2009). Sony introduced "Aibo" in late 1999; it was modeled after a dog and intended for companionship (Sony, n.d.). In 2002, iRobot introduced Roomba, a circular robot that vacuums floors (Kerr, 2013, November 29).

The Rise of Social Personal Robots

Many of the personal robots that were originally developed lacked bidirectional interaction between the user and robot (Campa, 2016). For instance, "Aibo" used sensors to mimic sounds and Roomba cleaned floors, but no bidirectional interaction took place. Presently, the trend is to develop personal service robots that allow for human-robot interaction (HRI) and bidirectional interaction.

As Breazeal (2002) noted "a new range of application domains (domestic, entertainment, health care, etc.) are driving the development of robots that can interact and cooperate with people as a partner, rather than as a tool" (p. 120). This development in technology is what many researchers call the rise of the social robot (Bartneck and Forlizzi, 2004). Bartneck and Forlizzi (2004) defined a social robot as "an autonomous or semi-autonomous robot that interacts and communicates with humans by following the behavioral norms expected by the people with whom the robot is intended to interact" (p. 592).

Numerous robots currently being developed to have some form of an HRI component are found in homes, schools, and hospitals (Bartneck and Forlizzi, 2004; Campa, 2016). These personal social robots assist people by performing a variety of important functions.

For example, "Buddy," developed by Blue Frog Robotics, is a personal social robot that can provide companionship, act as a personal assistant or provide home security. Some are used for educational applications such as assisting people in the autism spectrum (Blue Frog, n.d.; KPMG, 2016).

"Pepper," developed by SoftBank Robotics, "was designed to make its interaction with human beings as natural and intuitive as possible" (SoftBank Robotics, n.d.). Ideally, "Pepper" can detect emotions such as "joy, sadness, anger or surprise" (SoftBank Robotics, n.d.). Even products like Amazon's "Echo" were developed for social interaction. "Echo" is a voice-controlled household appliance that offers personal assistance for the user (Kim, 2016). "Echo" can play music, order food, check traffic patterns, the weather, and order groceries (Kim, 2016).

Forms of social personal robots can be found in the workplace, retirement homes, and hospitals; they are designed to assist customers and consumers. "Connie" was developed in a partnership between Hilton Hotels and IBM (International Business Machines) to offer concierge services (Thakur, 2017).

In Belgium, "Zora" was developed by Zora Bots to assist people in a healthcare setting. "Zora" is described as the first social robot used in health-care (Robotics Tomorrow, 2016). "Zora" "can lead a physical therapy class, read out TV programs, discuss weather forecasts, present local news," and entertain residents by teaching a dance class (Robotics Tomorrow, 2016). "Zora" and other service robots located in healthcare settings can provide reminders for people to take their medications or other daily reminders that are deemed important (Campa, 2016).

THE FUTURE OF PERSONAL SERVICE ROBOTS

Short Term

The present state of personal service robots is vast. They can assist people in a variety of tasks at home, work, and/or as a consumer (Bartneck and Forlizzi, 2004; Campa, 2016). Personal service robots will assist people with house cleaning, lawn mowing, pool cleaning, providing reminders, and various other activities. These devices will become more common in people's lives as technologies improve and the cost of these products become less expensive.

Personal service robots that have a social component will continue providing a variety of services such as giving reminders, making weather forecasts, providing healthcare coaching, and placing online orders. Knight (2015) and Mitchell (2015) both argued that social robots will be used for targeted purposes only and will lack the technological capacity to become true companions or to be used for physical activities, such as cooking.

As Basulto (2015) noted, many social robot functions can already be completed by a tablet device or smartphone, causing little incentive to purchase social personal service robots like "Buddy" or "Pepper" (Knight, 2015;

Mitchell, 2015). Conversely, social robots like "Echo," who are stationary and not expected to be a companion, will become commonplace over the next three to five years.

These devices will link different devices together, such as smartphones, smart refrigerators, and smart heating/cooling systems (Basulto, 2015; Mitchell, 2015). Overall, social robots will offer more interconnectedness and they will be more common in peoples' lives.

Mid Term

There will be more technological innovation during this time period that builds off the success of the previous inventions. To understand this transformation, in 2014, Pew Research (2014) asked over 1,800 experts in technology, the economy, and academia about what technological advancements did they expect to see by 2025. The majority of respondents argued that robotics would be intertwined with "nearly every aspect of daily life . . . from distant manufacturing processes to the most mundane household activities" (Pew Research, 2014, p. 19).

Stowe Boyd, a researcher for GigaOM Research, argued "X-rays will be reviewed by a batter of *Watson*-grade AIs . . ." (Pew Research, 2014, p. 19). Elizabeth Albrycht, a professor at the Paris School of Business, expected "by 2025 we may well be witnessing the disappearance of AI and robotics into the ordinary landscape as they follow the usual path of technology. First we see it, then it becomes invisible as it integrates into the landscape itself" (Pew Research, 2014, p. 22).

Hal Varian, an economist for Google, expected "in general, they [robots] will infer what we want, and our role is simply to refine and verify that expectation" (Pew Research, 2014, p. 24). Lastly, Jonathan Grudin, a researcher for Microsoft, expected "more robotic assistance for the elderly and infirm, because the demands are . . . increasing" (Pew Research, 2014, p. 27). In all, personal service robots will be the norm in the home and workplace, as more smart devices become interconnected.

As for personal service social robots, Brian Scassellati, a Yale University robotics professor, had a different argument. He contended that there will be limits over the next ten years because "social robots are not ready to become constant companions or even effective salespeople . . . they're going to be for targeted use, and probably not for the general population" (Knight, 2015).

His argument is that the technology has three major problems to overcome: capability, safety and cost (Walker, 2014). First, "Pepper," "Zora," and other social robots mishear words that lead to confusion and frustration by humans (Walker, 2014). Second, people may not feel safe to have robots in the home or use them in the workplace, such as a healthcare setting (Ambasna-Jones,

2016; Knight, 2015; Walker, 2014). Lastly, many researchers argue that personal social robots could be too expensive for the average consumer (Knight, 2015; Pew Research, 2014; Walker, 2014).

Thus, on one hand, people at home and work will use personal service robots that do not rely on a social component in their everyday life. On the other hand, service robots with a social component will be a growing trend as technological innovation occurs. These devices will need to have various issues solved before they become common in home or at work.

Long Term

Like the previous decade, technological innovation will occur, causing more people to acquire personal service robots; they may be commonly found in most households and workplaces. Moreover, like the previous decade, researchers will continue to deal with the challenges of technology and innovation before social robots are normal. As stated in the previous section, capability, cost, and safety are all issues that have to be solved (Walker, 2014).

In addition, one major obstacle that will influence the success of personal service robots will be the ability for researchers to solve the *uncanny valley*, which is the idea that humans seem to accept robots that do not look like a human. However, they have an inability to relate to robots that somewhat resemble humans. Further, they do not accept a robot as humanoid "until the resemblance is truly excellent" (Bekey, 2012, p. 25).

A design that is anything less than humanlike will result in people finding the robots repulsive and/or scary (Bekey, 2012; Yao, 2017). Thus, "a designer must either build a robot so humanlike as to be virtually indistinguishable from humans, or opt to be abstract" (Yao, 2017). In fact, this is one reason why personal service social robots avoid looking too humanlike; designers are attempting to evade the *uncanny valley*. Yao (2017) also noted that the *uncanny valley* applies to the functionality of all robots. As soon as they malfunction or mishear a command, humans get irritated and annoyed (Yao, 2017).

By the year 2040, personal service robots may be ubiquitous in the home and work. Humans may be in constant contact with their personal service robots and the majority of them will have some form of artificial intelligence. At home, humans will be able to control the majority of their devices through a handheld smart device.

Robots will be able to use a techno handshake to assess a person's emotional state, vital signs, and stress levels (Duffy, 2003). For work, personal service robots will be the norm. They will assist people in restaurants, hospitals, schools, hotels, and other major commerce areas. These robots may be as omnipresent as industrial robots are in a manufacturing setting.

MACHINE LEARNING AND DEEP LEARNING

Personal service robots stem from machine learning and deep learning. Machine learning is a method where a computer accesses data and based on statistical relationship, writes its own program (Ford, 2015). For example, an individual viewing books at barnesandnoble.com or Amazon.com will receive other recommended books to view based on their search requests. Ford (2015) argued that "[m]achine learning generally involves two steps: an algorithm is first trained on known data and is then unleashed to solve similar problems with new information" (p. 89).

Machine learning is the start of the machine extracting data on its own and learning to use that data to make decisions. There are numerous approaches to machine learning; however, according to Ford (2015), a powerful technique involves using artificial neural networks, which are systems designed to operate like the human brain. The technology is known as deep learning.

For instance, a deep learning system powers the speech recognition capability of Amazon's "Echo." Deep learning extends to the field of robotics as intelligent systems are designed and built to interact with humans in various tasks. Examples of personal service robots containing machine and deep learning systems are:

- "Connie," a robot concierge, designed by IBM and Hilton. "*Connie* is powered by *Watson*, a cognitive computing technology platform that represents a new era in computing where systems understand the world in the way that humans do—through senses, learning and experience" (Hilton, 2016, para. 4).
- "Miko," a companion robot is India's robot for children. "It is the first consumer robot, one can that can find a place in the family, to come from India. Replacing screen time with a more active companion that can help a child play, learn and grow" (Indian Moms Connect, 2017, para.6). The robot is equipped with a moral center powered by ancient Indian values and has a parental dashboard to customize and manage activity by child.
- "ElliQ" assists older adults with aging. The robot helps the aging population stay socially and physically active. "Thanks to machine learning, *ElliQ* can understand the user's personality, preferences, and habits. The robot can then suggest going for a walk, watching a TED talk, or contacting family members through Facebook Messenger" (Demaitre, 2017, para. 7).

THE IMPACT ON COMMUNITY COLLEGES

Community colleges are uniquely designed to train and educate the workforce. The institutions must be responsive to the growing and changing needs of local industry by offering current programs and services. Institutions must also research emerging career fields to ensure a sustainable local workforce as well as a sustainable college community.

Technology advancements have opened doors of new program offerings for the community college. According to Kahn (2016), "[t]echnology has not only created departments and jobs within companies, but created the need for entirely new companies and businesses" (para. 16). With personal service robots on the rise, community colleges are in a prime position to educate and train in the growing field of robotics.

The most common robotics curriculum in community colleges today is mechatronics, which is targeted to the manufacturing career field (R. Jones, personal communication, June 12, 2017). In many mechatronics programs, robotics courses are part of the program. In addition, with the increase of robots and personal service robots, many community colleges will need to develop a robotics and personal robotics curriculum.

Short Term

Over the next three years, community colleges will begin to grow their robotics programs as they incorporate and design mechatronics programs. The majority of community colleges will incorporate robotics into programs like mechatronics and other technical programs.

Moreover, community colleges that offer robotics curricula can have an important role with personal service robots. They can design programs that assist with servicing the robots. Individuals interested in the study of personal service robots can choose their area based on three core parts of every robot: (a) body, (b) nervous system, (c) brain (Owen-Hill, 2015).

Each part requires a specific area of academic study, such as, the body would require Mechanical Engineering, the nervous system would need Electrical and Electronic Engineering and the brain would require Computer Science (Owen-Hill, 2015). Mechanical Engineering involves assisting engineers in the design, development, and testing of the robot body.

Electrical and Electronic Engineering involves working with engineers in designing, evaluating, troubleshooting, and repairing the electronics of the robot nervous system. Computer Science involves the software and software systems of the robot brain (Owen-Hill, 2015). Community colleges could offer careers in the following categories:

- Technician - There are several types of technicians. A robotics technician could repair and maintain robots and build robotic parts along with other tasks. An electromechanical technician works with the engineer in the design process of new robots (Calhoun Community College, 2017).

• Operators - At present, every robot has to have operators who oversee it 24 hours a day. Should anything go wrong or break down, an operator needs to be on top of the situation immediately. Working in shifts around the clock, the operators ensure that everything goes smoothly. The technology associated with robotics is growing. More and more robots will replace humans in everyday tasks and jobs creating the need for more and more robotics engineers, technicians, and others in the field on the rise (Calhoun Community College, 2017).

Currently, there are community colleges that are already designing curricula that include robotics courses, such as Greenville Technical College in Greenville, South Carolina; Alamance Community College in Graham, North Carolina; and Edmonds Community College in Lynnwood, Washington. The current trend offering of robotics in community colleges is limited to one or two courses embedded into a degree; however, this beginning reveals that community colleges are moving toward the emerging trend of robotics in society.

Mid Term

Nudelman and Szoldra (2015) list several industries that will be transformed by robots by the year 2025, as shown in Table 2. The influx of robots into these industries is an opportunity for the community college to include more robotics offerings in these career fields. Community colleges can also explore the use of robots as a method of teaching in the classroom. One example is a face-to-face class, which includes students who join the class remotely by use of a robot stand-in.

> The device looks like a small Segway with an iPad attached to the top. Distance students meanwhile login and choose which robot they want to use (each has its own name, such as Aristotle or Rosa Parks). The "robot" students can then view their classmates through the video screen and also control the device to move around the classroom or turn to face their peers (Johnson, 2017).

Another robot, "Kubi," features a small stand for iPads. Remote users turn their screens to face in-person students. These robots, utilized in the classroom, offer an alternative method for class participation. With the increase of robotics in the eight industries, new program offerings can utilize the robots to meet increased enrollment numbers.

It is predicted that industrial robots will transform the following industries by 2025: Aerospace, Agriculture, Artificial Intelligence, Automotive, Finance, Healthcare, and Manufacturing. (Nudelman and Szoldra, 2015).

Furthermore, during this time period, community colleges will embed and design robotics maintenance in various programs. Even though community colleges traditionally do not offer Mechanical Engineering or Electrical and Electronic Engineering, they can embed maintenance programs in their mechatronics program, engineering technology program, or pre-engineering program.

These programs will focus on programming, troubleshooting, repairing the electronics (i.e., the nervous system), repairing the body, and assist with software maintenance of personal robots. Moreover, if robots are going to be found in the workplace and at home, community colleges need to create programs to service them. They are in the best position to design curriculum to train employees to work on industrial robots and personal robots.

Long Term

To stay relevant, community colleges must adapt to the future needs of students as they continue to provide programs and services in robotics. They can do this by adapting their curricula to meet the demands of the business community and the local economic development organization. Community colleges will develop and offer robotics programs that assist with the maintenance of robots and personal robots.

More importantly, community colleges will offer courses and degrees in robotics. No longer will these courses be part of another curriculum, but they will have their own program. In fact, these programs will be as common as biotechnology, nursing, and radiology are today.

BUILDING PARTNERSHIPS BETWEEN BUSINESSES AND COMMUNITY COLLEGES

According to Spangler (2002), the elements that make up the seeds of a partnership are shared mission and goals, common activities, growing strategically with a good company, economic opportunity, and leveraged resources. There are two questions that must be asked for successful partnerships to occur. They are: 1) what areas of training need addressing? 2) can the institution align with the company's needs? (J. Howard, personal communication, August 2, 2016).

Ford (2015) makes the case for a guaranteed income since the job market continues to erode because of the technology-driven inequality. If the assumption is that machines and robots will eventually replace human labor to a certain degree, then it is suggested that purchasing power should be redistributed for economic growth to continue.

If machines and robots were to substitute for workers entirely, then no one would have a job or an income from any type of labor (Ford, 2015). However, there will always be the need for humans to creatively design, probably with the help of robots, the human culture to develop further, most likely into areas we do not even conceive today. These new areas may provide jobs that do not exist at present.

Community colleges will probably remain a leader in training, educating, and giving students on-the-job experiences, which prepares them to compete for good jobs in automation and robotics. Building partnerships between businesses and community colleges is going to be vital today, in the near future, and beyond.

Community colleges must continue to develop creative ways to establish relationships with the business community, specifically, with those using or developing robotics. Community colleges should partner with local businesses to develop appropriate training and academic curricula, which meets local workforce needs and the ability to detect and respond to changes (Friend, 2010).

This also suggests community colleges should partner with local educational institutions to deliver comprehensive training (Friend, 2010). Partnering with business and industries will amplify student career opportunities.

In comparison to the seven billion people on Earth, there are only 1.2 billion full-time, formal jobs in the world (Clifton, 2011). This situation is going to place much stress on the United States and other countries for future job creations. Ford (2015) argued that job automation is a primary threat to workers who have little education and lower-skill levels.

Since most jobs are routine and repetitive, technology will assist machines to take on jobs that are predictable in workplace tasks. This also will place an enormous amount of stress on both the economy and society (Ford, 2015). Community colleges, by partnering with businesses and industries, can address these issues the United States will encounter in the future.

Community colleges will need to partner with business and industry to create a continually changing skilled workforce needed to compete in the global marketplace. For community colleges and businesses to stay relevant and grow, partnerships will need to be created and maintained.

One can predict that community colleges will have an impact on the robotics industry in the future. There are numerous reasons why community colleges are an excellent choice for science and engineering students. They have low tuition costs, are close to home, and offer open enrollment. Clearly these are all attractive qualities to many students who will become vital components in the future workforce. Without a doubt, community colleges are a viable, successful option for science and engineering students (Calhoun Community College, 2017).

CONCLUSION

Research reveals an increase in home and personal service robots by 2020 (Kharpal, 2015). These robots have the ability to interact with people to provide home security, companionship, education, or to assist customers and consumers. As technology continues to build on previous inventions, personal service robots will move toward the norm in households and the workplace by 2025. By year 2040, personal service robots will be ubiquitous in the home and the workplace.

The emerging trend of robots in society impacts the community college. Therefore, community colleges must be proactive in developing robotics curricula. Over the next three years, community colleges will need to incorporate robotics into many, if not all, of its program offerings.

By 2025, robots will transform other industries, which lead to robotics maintenance embedded into programs. Community colleges can also explore the use of robots in teaching methodologies as an alternate method for remote student participation. By 2040, stand-alone robotics programs in community colleges will most likely be as common as nursing programs are today.

As community colleges lead the way in training and education for robotics, building partnerships with businesses is vital. In future years, community colleges will address job creation needs in the United States through partnerships with business and industry resulting in a more globally competitive community.

REFERENCES

Ambasna-Jones, M. (2016, May 9). *How social robots are dispelling myths and caring for humans.* https://www.theguardian.com/media-network/2016/may/09/robots-social-health-care-elderly-children.

Bartneck, C., & Forlizzi, J. (2004). A Design-Centered Framework for Social Human-Robot Interaction. *Proceedings of the ROMAN Conference,* 591–594.

Basulto, D. (2015, July 21). *Why social robots could be coming soon to a home near you.* https://www.washingtonpost.com/news/innovations/wp/2015/07/21/why-social-robots-could-be-coming-soon-to-a-home-near-you/?utm_term=.d6f493117d34.

Bekey, G. (2012). Current trends in robotics: Technology and ethics. In *Robot ethics: The ethical and social implications of robotics,* 17–34. Cambridge, MA: MIT Press.

Blue Frog Robotics. (n.d.). *About Buddy.* http://www.bluefrogrobotics.com/en/buddy/.

Breazeal, C. (2002). Emotion and sociable humanoid robots. *International Journal of Human-Computer Studies, 59,* 119–155.

Calhoun Community College. (2017). *Robotics / Mechatronics.* www.calhoun.edu/academics/technologies/robotics-mechatronics.

Campa, R. (2016). The rise of social robots: A review of the recent literature. *Journal of Evolution and Technology, 26*(1), 106–113.

Clifton, Jim. (2011). *The coming jobs war.* New York: Gallup Press.

Dahl, T. S., & Boulos, M. N. K. (2013). Robots in health and social care: A complementary technology to home care and telehealthcare. *Robotics 3*(1), 1–21.

Demaitre, E. (2017). *ElliQ robot wants to ease aging in place.* http://www.robotic-strends.com/article/elliq_robot_wants_to_ease_aging_in_place/personal.

Duffy, B. (2003). Anthropomorphism and the social robot. *Robotics and Autonomous Systems, 42,* 177–190.

Ford, M. (2015). *Rise of the robots: technology and the threat of a jobless future.* New York: Basic Books.

Friend, E. (2010). Partnering with Business Amplifies Students' Career Opportunities. *Tech Directions, 70*(3), 19–21.

Hegel, F., Muhl, C., Wrede, B., Hielscher-Fastabend, M., & Sagerer, G. (2009). Understanding Social Robots. *Second International Conference on Advances in Computer-Human Interactions (ACHI),* 169–174.

Hilton. (2016). *Hilton and IBM Pilot "Connie," the world's first Watson-enabled hotel concierge domain.* https://www-03.ibm.com/press/us/en/pressrelease/49307. wss.

Indian Moms Connect. (2017). *India's first companion robot for children is here!* http://www.indianmomsconnect.com/2017/02/16/indias-first-companion-robot-children/.

International Federation of Robotics. (2016). *Classification of service robots by application areas.* https://ifr.org/img/office/Service_Robots_Chapter_1_2.pdf.

International Federation of Robotics. (2016). *Executive Summary: World robotics 2016 service robots.* https://ifr.org/downloads/press/02_2016/Executive_Summary_Service_Robots_2016.pdf.

Johnson, S. (2017). *Robot students? College classrooms try letting far-away students attend via remote-control stand-in.* https://www.edsurge.com/news/2017-05-11-robot-students-college-classrooms-try-letting-far-away-students-attend-via-remote-control-stand-in.

Kahn, M. (2016). *Robots won't just take jobs, they'll create them.* https://techcrunch.com/2016/05/13/robots-wont-just-take-jobs-theyll-create-them/.

Kerr, J. (2013, November 29). *The history of the Roomba.* http://fortune.com/2013/11/29/the-history-of-the-roomba/.

Kharpal, A. (2015, December 15). *1 in 10 Americans to have robots in home by 2020.* http://www.cnbc.com/2015/12/16/1-in-10-americans-to-have-robots-in-home-by-2020.html.

Kim, E. (2016, April 2). *The inside story of how Amazon created Echo, the next billion-dollar business no one saw coming.* http://www.businessinsider.com/the-inside-story-of-how-amazon-created-echo-2016-4.

KPMG Management Consulting. (2016). *Social robots.* https://assets.kpmg.com/content/dam/kpmg/pdf/2016/06/social-robots.pdf.

Knight, W. (2015, September 16). *A Japanese robot is learning the American way.* https://www.technologyreview.com/s/541171/a-japanese-robot-is-learning-the-american-way/.

Knight, W. (2015, July 24). *Personal robots: artificial friends with limited benefits.* https://www.technologyreview.com/s/539356/personal-robots-artificial-friends-with-limited-benefits/.

Lin, P. (2012). Introduction to robot ethics. In *Robot ethics: The ethical and social implications of robotics*, 3–15. Cambridge, MA: MIT Press.

Mitchell, D. (2015, May 15). *Household robots are here, but where are they going?* https://www.technologyreview.com/s/537701/household-robots-are-here-but-where-are-they-going/.

Nudelman, M., & Szoldra, P. (2015). *Eight industries robots will transform by year 2025.* http://www.businessinsider.com/8-industries-robots-will-completely-transform-by-2025-2015-12.

Owen-Hill, A. (2015). *What to study for a career in robotics?* http://blog.robotiq.com/what-to-study-for-a-career-in-robotics.

Robotics Tomorrow. (2016, April 12). *The first social robot already widely used in healthcare.* http://www.roboticstomorrow.com/article/2016/04/zora-the-first-social-robot-already-widely-used-in-healthcare/7927.

Smith, A., & Anderson, J. (2014, August 6). AI, robotics and the future of jobs. http://www.pewinternet.org/2014/08/06/future-of-jobs/.

SoftBank Robotics. (n.d.). *Who is Pepper?* https://www.ald.softbankrobotics.com/en/cool-robots/pepper.

Sony. (n.d.). *Aibos history.* http://www.sony-aibo.com/aibos-history/.

Spangler, M. S. (2002). Concluding observations on successful partnerships. In M. Spangler (ed.), *Developing Successful Partnerships with Business and Community*, 77–80. San Francisco, CA: Jossey Bass.

Thakur, A. (2017, May 9). *Robots are changing not just the way we work but parenting as well; here's a glance at what the future holds.* http://economictimes.indiatimes.com/magazines/panache/between-the-lines/robots-are-changing-not-just-the-way-we-work-but-parenting-as-well-heres-a-glance-of-what-the-future-holds/articleshow/58595268.cms.

Walker, M. (2014, April). *Ready or not: Here come social robots.* https://www.wired.com/insights/2013/04/ready-or-not-here-come-personal-robots/.

Yao, M. (2017, February 13). *Why building social robots is much harder than you think.* http://www.topbots.com/building-social-robots-jibo-anki-cozmo-much-harder-think/.

Chapter 3

3D Printing

Shakitha Barner, Takeem L. Dean, and Carlos McCormick

"Every sufficiently advanced technology seems like magic."

—Arthur C. Clarke

"The origins of 3D printing can be traced back to 1986, when the first patent was issued for stereolithography apparatus (SLA) by Charles (Chuck) Hull, who first invented his SLA machine in 1983" (Barnatt, 2016, p. 96). Briana Fishbein, Sales Operations Manager at #d Systems stated,

> The company helps every sector that is can. We can create parts for manufacturing companies, dental molds for dentistry, or even 3D versions of architectural designs. We can make it and we can make it much faster than it could be made years ago (B. Fishbein, personal communication, May 5, 2017).

With the 3D printing of today, manufacturing companies are saving money; science and healthcare have more affordable options for people, and technical and community colleges have a new trade to offer students. This phenomenon is changing the way people live and providing a boost to the economy simultaneously.

WHAT IS 3D PRINTING?

"3D printers fabricate objects by controlling the placement and adhesion of successive layers of a build material in 3D space" (Barnatt, 2016, p. 3). "To start the process, one would create a virtual design known as a computer aided design (CAD) file" (B. Fishbein, personal communication, May 10, 2017).

> To 3D print an object, a digital model first needs to exist in a computer. . . . Once it is ready to be fabricated it needs to be put through some "slicing software"

that will divide it into a great many cross-sectional layers that are typically about 0.1 mm thick. These digital slivers are then sent to a 3D printer that fabricates them, one on top of the other, until they are built up into a complete 3D printed object (Barnatt, 2016, p. 3).

The 3D printing industry has expanded considerably over the years. Already seven different processes of 3D printing exist: material jetting, binder jetting, powder bed fusion, directed energy deposition, sheet lamination, material extrusion and vat photopolymerization (Matulka & Greene, 2014). These different processes allow the 3D printing industry to have a major impact on a variety of industries.

IMPACT OF 3D PRINTING

3D printing presents ways to assist businesses in various functions. The many facets of 3D printing provide benefits and challenges to all sectors that use it. "The 3D printer is an adaptation of Computer Numeric Controlled (CNC) machines that were invented in 1952 when researchers at Massachusetts Institute of Technology wired an early computer to a milling machine" (Martin, Bowden, and Merrill, 2014, p. 31).

3D printing continues to be of major interest; however, there are some concerns regarding its existence (Martin, et al., 2014). "For example, 3D printers have been linked to the design and manufacture of unregulated firearms" (Martin et al., 2014, p. 31). Furthermore, 3D printing presents a variety of learning curves (Martin, et al., 2014). Its evolution will continue to present benefits and challenges.

Science and Healthcare

3D printing is revolutionizing science; the medical field is utilizing the technology in various spectrums. Healthcare studies, for instance, argue 3D printing improves communications between the doctor and the patient: "Improving patient education by use of personalized 3D printed models appears to be a promising way to efficiently enhance the quality of personal exchange between a patient and his surgeon and influence overall patient satisfaction" (Bernhard et al., 2016, p. 343). Furthermore, scientists, like Dr. Arthur Olson, a molecular biologist, are using 3D printing technologies to explore Human Immunodeficiency Virus (HIV), the virus that causes AIDS (Live Science, 2014).

Over time, 3D printing technology cost is expected to decrease drastically which will allow sectors like healthcare to have the most recent devices on site. 3D printers on a hospital campus provide several benefits, such as medical research capabilities. Moreover, hospitals and doctors are excited about the opportunity to create their own instruments: "This technology is capable of manufacturing low-cost and customizable surgical devices, like 3D models for use in preoperative planning and surgical education and fabricated biomaterials" (Youssef, Spradling, Yoon, Dolan, Chamberlin, Okhunov, and Landman, 2016, p. 697).

Additionally, 3D printing is proving instrumental in enhancing the quality of life for humans. For example, medical professionals are using 3D manufactured human parts, like kidneys and livers, to prolong the life expectancy of individuals (Bernhard et al., 2016).

Other Uses of 3D Printing

According to Christopher Barnatt (2016),

> in the brave new world of 3D printing, it is now possible to make things that were previously impossible to manufacture. For example, a 3D printer can make a chain or necklace made up of links that do not have a break in them, and which will therefore never come apart at a seam (p. 20).

In other words, if something can be designed, no matter how complex, 3D printing can most likely produce it using its layer-by-layer process.

Other possibilities already completed are entire automobile bodies, internal parts of the engine and other parts of the car. If the design exists, there are 3D processes combined with the proper metal or plastic that can develop the product to whatever quality is needed.

Countries all over the world, such as Russia, the United Kingdom, United States, and Belgium, are getting into 3D processing of goods. By 2020 most likely millions of people will have flown on aircraft containing 3D printed parts (Barnatt, 2016). China has begun serious work on 3D processing of entire houses using layers of cement. This method could have a strong impact on the housing market in that country and internationally.

In 2012 the global market for 3D products was worth about $2.2 billion. By 2015 the dollar amount increased to $5.1 billion (Barnatt, 2016). Where the market is going is anyone's guess, but it seems to be on an exponential curve into the future. As that happens, tremendous changes will affect manufacturing in particular.

> Just as in the 1980s and 1990s, the personal computer rose up to drive the future of computing, so it remains possible that the personal 3D printing market will

become the most important driver for industrial 3D printing innovation in the decades ahead (Barnatt, 2016, p. 167).

3D printing is a construction method that has the potential to affect human beings on a great number of fronts. The development will most likely increase in speed and number of products as the process goes mainstream in an exponential manner.

COMMUNITY COLLEGE EDUCATION

The connection between 3D printing and science is not a new novelty; truthfully, Bernhard et al., (2016) points out the connection is nearly twenty years in the making. However, the relationship between 3D printing and education is still in its early stages. It is up to educational entities, specifically community colleges, to realize this phenomenon can have a major impact in education and take steps to develop training for entrepreneurs and students who are attracted to it.

Wake Technical Community College

In 2014, Wake Technical Community College (WTCC), located in Raleigh, North Carolina, received a National Science Foundation grant to integrate 3D printing at the college: "Wake Tech is at the forefront of 3D printing technology. This grant will allow the college to develop teaching and training methods that will provide highly-skilled workers to the industry and Wake County competitive" (Wake Technical Community College, 2014).

One of the grant objectives is to implement 3D printing in Science, Technology, Engineering, and Math programming. In Mechanical Engineering Technology, for example, 3D printing is affording students the opportunity to convert their 2D drawings into 3D prototypes. Additionally, the 3D printing allows students to test their projects: "When students are just designing it on the computers and they cannot put their hands on it, because it is abstract, but as soon as they can print and play with the object they are instantly engaged" (D. Adams, personal communication, May 22, 2017).

In the next five to ten years. Community college leaders, like Dana Adams, WTCC 3D printing instructor, believe institutions will need to implement 3D printing concepts at various levels of the college (personal communication, May 22, 2017). Ultimately, students will be able to experience a physical aspect to learning, which will benefit them upon graduation.

The reasoning behind such lofty expectations is the fact 3D printing promotes student success: "The main emphasis in allowing learners access to

Additive Manufacturing technologies is to provide and expose students to long term progress and innovative thinking" (Beer, 2013, p. 34). At present many community colleges are in the midst of turbulent times concerning financial support and are being asked to demonstrate student success. As a result, it is vital institutions explore various technologies that will promote access, retention, and student success.

Dr. Andrew Vinal, WTCC Science instructor, notes, "3D printing helps personalize what I do because a significant amount of my instruction revolves around molecules. The 3D physical molecule allows students to visualize and conceptualize what I am teaching" (A. Vinal, personal communication, May 4, 2017). According to Vinal, student comprehension is drastically improved when students utilize a 3D model (A. Vinal, personal communication, May 4, 2017).

Sierra College

Sierra College, a two-year institution, is implementing a variety of 3D printing science courses: "We are creating curriculum programs in courses, like Anthropology, Biological Sciences, and Chemistry" (Beer, 2013, p. 36). It is evident educational entities, such as community colleges, need to integrate 3D printing in course curricula.

However, expanding 3D printing in education over the next ten years potentially can be a challenge: "This is a challenging concept due to the fact that the technology continues to evolve at such a rapid pace" (Beer, 2013, p. 36). Instructor Adams agrees with the aforementioned statement; however, she believes community colleges are better positioned to handle the speed.

> In four-year programs they want to hammer in theory. At community colleges, we are more adaptable to industry needs because we are so focused on jobs after graduation; as a result, we are easily able to pull in new technologies into our program (Adams, personal communication, May 22, 2017).

3D Printing Courses

It is imperative community colleges constantly evolve. Institutions that remain status quo and fail to strategically plan for the future will rapidly become obsolete. One strategy for success is creating innovative and dynamic courses. Researchers believe academia should heavily invest in creating programs that evolve around STEM careers (Beer, 2013). Already some students are coming to community colleges with hands-on experience with 3D printing from middle and high school, and they are seeking the same educational experience (Lacey, 2010).

Economic Engine

The 3D printing industry itself is developing exponentially; thus, it is having a major economic impact on the world. Keeney (2016) believes the current economics for the 3D printing industry is $5.2 billion dollars, and she expects the aforementioned figure to balloon to $490 billion by the year 2025. As a result of the statistics mentioned above, community colleges in three to five years, most certainly, will need to have various 3D printing programs interconnected in institutional programs.

Florence-Darlington Technical College (FDTC), located in Florence, South Carolina, is considered an early adopter in terms of integrating 3D printing in education. The college offers 3D printing in vocational and college transfer courses. The leadership at FDTC is aware of the exponential development of 3D printing and is getting in the process early on.

As noted earlier, the current economic impact for 3D printing is $5.2 billion (Keeney, 2016). Because of FDTC's forward thinking mentality, the college is well positioned in this billion dollar industry. In fact, the college is partnering with local and global companies providing 3D services. According to David Bonner, Director Additive Manufacturing, FDTC, the college expects to receive $400,000 this academic year from businesses for products created at the college (D. Bonner, personal communication, May 11, 2017).

General Electric Medical is one of several clients for which the institution performs services. Thus, the college is keeping pace with trends in economy: "From simple yet revolutionary inventions like the wheel and gears, to complex manufactured products like cell phones and track shores, engineering is defined the way society moves and evolves" (Lacey, 2010, p. 19). 3D printing may seem complicated; however, its benefits are straightforward.

Future Impact of 3D Printing

Human tissue engineering is on the horizon. "Advances in 3D printing and medical technology will soon make it possible to construct human tissue in a lab, implant it in a patient and watch it grow into the body" (Mellgard, 2017). Furthermore, medical imaging and 3D printing will eventually become integrated. "At the hospital, data from preoperative imaging studies will be converted into CAD files for creating personalized surgical models and patient-specific surgical devices" (Youssef et al., 2016, p. 701). Within the next decade or so, 3D printing will be "saving and improving human lives using personalized medical devices printed by a machine" (Mellgard).

The pricing of 3D printers has dramatically decreased over time. Consider in 2009, *The Economist* announced the future launch of a less than $5000 3D printer; four years later, the same source was reporting on how competition and expiry of early patents brought the price of 3D printers below $1000 (Bernhard et al., 2016, p. 344). The lowering costs of 3D printers and the increasing use of them will benefit the healthcare field greatly.

IMPACT ON THE COMMUNITY COLLEGE

Short Term

The future of 3D printing in education is bright. During the next five to ten years, researchers expect this multibillion dollar industry to be in every sector of education (Beer, 2013). Community colleges are in a great position to benefit from this phenomenon.

Even though in recent years community colleges nationally have experienced declines in enrollment, 3D printing is a technology that potentially could help reverse declining numbers. Wake Technical Community College, for example, notes student enrollment in Mechanical Engineering is increasing, as a result of implementing 3D printing programming (D. Adams, personal communication, May 22, 2013).

3D printing course offerings at community colleges can be offered in continuing education programs or as a part of other degree programs. "3D printing will probably not be an entire program at a community college but it's possible to become a great training tool for the continuing education program" (B. Fishbein, personal communication, May 10, 2017). Although 3D printing has a lot of components, it may not become a full degree, certificate, or diploma program specifically for that technology. However Continuing Education will benefit greatly from teaching individuals how to use this technology.

Mid Term

Two-year institutions rely significantly on partnerships. As noted earlier, the landscape of 3D printing is blossoming and is going to continue to expand opening the door for community colleges to develop a multitude of partnerships. For example, educational institutions are already taking full advantage of this opportunity to collaborate:

> A partnership between the Commonwealth of Virginia, University of Virginia, and the City of Charlottesville has led to the creation of Commonwealth Engineering and Design Academy at Buford Middle School, a new type of school built specifically around project-based learning with the help of new technologies, such as 3-D printing (Beer, 2013, p. 35).

York Technical College (YTC) in Rock Hill, South Carolina, created a partnership with 3D Systems when the company opened a new location in the service area of the college. YTC provided the training for employees, and the company provided jobs for the community (D. King, personal communication, May 8, 2017).

3D technology is a tool that instructors from various curriculums will gradually integrate, as it has proven to increase the success rate of students in the classroom (A. Vinal, personal communication, May 4, 2017). "With 3D printing, technology students can create models from digital information without needing either the skills or equipment that had previously been used to create professional models of products" (Samuels and Flowers, 2015, p. 17). "Projects that involve 3D printing both educate and motivate technology students. They teach students processes used in today's industry for product design and manufacturing" (Lacey, 2010, p. 17).

"Indeed, 3D printing offers a fun and interesting way of fostering engineering and manufacturing skills in the technology and engineering classroom" (Samuels and Flowers, 2015, p. 22). "The process of using 3D printing technology can both excite and empower technology and engineering students" (Samuels and Flowers, 2015, p. 25).

Long Term

Although 3D printing is becoming more popular, at present it is not enough for community colleges to develop an entire program for it; however, 3D printing technology can enhance several programs. For instance, Machine Tool is a program that will soon need to incorporate 3D printing technology.

The 3D printers are faster, easier, and less laborious than traditional enhanced technology printers. 3D printing technology will enhance the education programs because future teachers will need to know the technology that will be in their classrooms. Learning this technology in college will allow for a better experience in the field.

COMMUNITY COLLEGE LEADERSHIP

Leaders in community colleges should be thinking about 3D printing and how it will affect local businesses, their college, and the services that are offered to students. Community college administration should include 3D printers in their capital budgets. Without it, the college will not be leading in innovation but falling behind rapidly.

Chief Academic Officers should be challenging all technical and non-technical areas to find a place for the incorporation of 3D printing technology.

Without this college-wide initiative, the institution faces the possibility of getting too far behind the exponential curve to catch up.

Institutions with 3D printers can build better partnerships with local and regional businesses by incorporating the technology in presentations. For example, during construction of a new building, colleges could allow an architect to work with students to create a 3D visual of the building. Then, instead of deciphering 2D drawings, donors will be better able to envision the project and, therefore, may be more willing to contribute generously. The ability to show partners that the college has the same high-level technology as other entities will promote donations.

CONCLUSION

Technology is evolving at an exponential pace. Thus, as 3D printing, which is already appearing in high school and community college classrooms, becomes more prevalent, it is important for community colleges to stay ahead of the research and best practices. Community college leaders will need someone on the faculty who is an expert in 3D printing to help keep the college abreast of new findings relevant to this new phenomenon.

Community colleges will need to expand their course offerings in 3D printing to address the demands of students coming to campus wanting to learn how to manufacture the devices. This era of the evolution of 3D printing is a prime time for community colleges to reconsider their purpose to meet the needs of today's and tomorrow's technology demands.

REFERENCES

Barnatt, C. (2016). *3D Printing*. Printed and bound on demand.

Beer, N. (2013). Industry Evaluation and Recommendation Report. California.

Bernhard, J. C., Isotani, S., Matsugasumi, T., Duddalwar, V., Hung, A. J., Suer, E., & Hu, B. (2016). Personalized 3D printed model of kidney and tumor anatomy: A useful tool for patient education. *World journal of urology*, *34*(3), 337–345.

Keeney. T. (2016). *3D Printing Market: Analysts Are Underestimating the Future*. https://ark-invest.com/research/3d-printing-market.

Lacey, G. (2010). Get Students Excited—3D Printing Brings Designs to Life. *Tech Directions*, *70*(2), 17–19.

Live Science. (2014). *Scientist using 3D-printed models to study biological molecules*. http://www.foxnews.com/health/2014/12/30/scientists-using-3d-printed-models-to-study-biological-molecules.html.

Martin, R. L., Bowden, N. S., & Merrill, C. (2014). 3D Printing in Technology and Engineering Education. *Technology and Engineering Teacher*, *73*(8), 30–35.

Matulka, R., & Greene, M. (2014, June 19). How 3D Printers Work. https://energy.gov/articles/how-3d-printers-work.

Mellgard, Peter. Medical 3-D Printing Will 'Enable a New Kind of Future'. *The World Post*. http://www.huffingtonpost.com/peter-mellgard/medical-3d-printing-future_b_7088994.html.

Samuels, K., & Flowers, J. (2015). 3D Printing: Exploring Capabilities. *Technology and Engineering Teacher*, *74*(7), 17–21.

Wake Technical Community College. (2014). U.S. Representative David Price announces major grant for Wake Tech. http://www.waketech.edu/news/us-rep-david-price-announces-major-grant-award-wake-tech-0#.WR2WRuErKUk.

Youssef, R. F., Spradling, K., Yoon, R., Dolan, B., Chamberlin, J., Okhunov, Z., & Landman, J. (2016). Applications of three-dimensional printing technology in urological practice. *BJU international*, *116*(5), 697–702.

Chapter 4

Autonomous Vehicles and Drones

Charlotte Blackwell, Amy Davis, and Cristy Holmes

"Today's cars are brainless."

—Hod Lipson

This chapter provides an explanation of how autonomous vehicles and drones work, the benefits and challenges of implementing these technologies, and predictions of the technological impacts on the future of community colleges and its leadership. The technology for autonomous drones and vehicles deployment in the United States is quickly approaching an implementation phase.

"When the Defense Advanced Research Projects Agency (DARPA) launched their first Grand Challenge in 2004, the idea of autonomous driverless vehicles for everyone seemed like a plot for a bad science fiction novel about the far distant future" (Frey, 2015, p. 40). However, in less than a decade the idea became a reality.

As the operational technology for autonomous drones and vehicles rapidly evolves, several challenges exist for full deployment of these technologies, thus potentially slowing down the process. Because generous benefits exist for the continued development of autonomous drones and vehicles, the challenges of safety and regulatory issues will remain prominent foci for states, the federal government, engineers and technology developers in the near future.

AUTONOMOUS DRONES AND VEHICLES

Drones

Drones, also known as unmanned aerial systems (UAVs), fly both with limited human control and autonomously without human interaction. While the origin of drone development dates back to World War I when the United States developed an aerial torpedo for launching an attack on the enemy (Aquino-Segarra, 2016), by the early twenty-first century the evolution of drone technology expanded far beyond military usage.

Today, drones provide data analysis, delivery, and inspection tasks "for commercial, industrial and agriculture purposes, and law enforcement" (Aquino-Segarra, 2016, p. 338). Specifically, several of today's industries use drones for tasks such as package delivery, filming of aerial footage, monitoring construction progress, conducting scientific research, and covering breaking news stories.

While drones typically serve a purpose for commercial or other industries, the popularity of operating a drone as a personal hobby is exploding. In fact, the Federal Aviation Administration (FAA) predicts that small model hobbyist fleet of unmanned aircraft systems will more than triple in size from 1.1 million vehicles in 2016 to 3.55 million units in 2021.

"The average annual growth rate over the five-year forecast period is 26.4 percent" (Price, 2017, p. 6). Incidentally, the FAA predicts "the commercial, non-hobbyist fleet is forecast to grow from 42,000 in 2016 to 442,000 in 2021. The average annual growth rate over the five-year forecast period is 58.6 percent" (Price, 2017, p. 7).

Having an understanding of how drones operate is fundamental to make connections for involvement in supportive roles and partnerships regarding this technology. A variety of drone sizes exist with larger drones used mostly for military purposes and smaller drones for civilian tasks.

The drone can consist of different technologies, such as infrared cameras, GPS and laser systems. It operates by remote control through a ground crew (Corrigan, 2017). Gyroscope stabilization technology "provides essential navigational information to the central slight controller" (Corrigan, 2017, p. 1), which acts as the central brain of the drone.

Drones operate with FPV (First Person View), meaning "a video camera is mounted on the unmanned aerial vehicle and broadcasts the live video to the pilot on the ground so the pilot is flying the aircraft as if he/she was on-board the aircraft instead of looking at the craft from the pilot's actual ground position" (Corrigan, 2017, p. 1). A bevy of other complexities comprises a UAV such as motor, battery, propellers and frame types.

Autonomous Vehicles

The technology and concept of autonomous vehicles, also referred to as self-driving or driverless cars and trucks, provides a highly scientific alternative to the entire concept of personal automobile transportation. This revolutionary technology will ultimately transform the auto and truck industry.

Self-driving vehicles will revolutionize how people, goods, and services move from one place to another; thus, affecting future transportation planning decisions, such as roadway design, parking costs, and public transit demand (DeAngelis, 2016). Self-driving technology provides great potential to enhance public safety, provide mobility for the elderly and disabled, reduce traffic congestion, improve environmental quality, and advance transportation efficiency (Self-Driving Coalition for Safer Streets, 2017).

To understand the evolution of autonomous vehicle technology, the National Highway Traffic Safety Administration (NHTSA), a division of the US Department of Transportation, outlined the six levels of autonomous vehicles as classified by SAE International, a global association of engineers and related technical experts in the aerospace, automotive and commercial-vehicle industries:

- *Level 0 - No Automation*: The full-time performance by the human driver of all aspects of the dynamic driving task, even when enhanced by warning or intervention systems
- *Level 1 - Driver Assistance*: The driving mode specific execution by a driver assistance system of either steering or acceleration/deceleration using information about the driving environment and with the expectation that the human driver performs all remaining aspects of the dynamic driving task
- *Level 2 - Partial Automation*: The driving mode specific execution by one or more driver assistance systems of both steering and acceleration/deceleration using information about the driving environment and with the expectation that the human driver performs all remaining aspects of the dynamic driving task
- *Level 3 - Conditional Automation*: The driving mode specific performance by an Automated Driving System of all aspects of the dynamic driving task with the expectation that the human driver will respond appropriately to a request to intervene
- *Level 4 - High Automation*: The driving mode specific performance by an Automated Driving System of all aspects of the dynamic driving task, even if a human driver does not respond appropriately to a request to intervene
- *Level 5 - Full Automation*: The full-time performance by an Automated Driving System of all aspects of the dynamic driving task under all roadway and environmental conditions that can be managed by a human driver (SAE International, 2016)

Currently, the automobile industry operates at Level 1 with some automation features such as cruise control, obstruction warning, and parallel parking (Litman, 2017). Manufacturers such as Tesla now offer Level 2 such as lane guidance and accident avoidance. A focused effort by Google to test cars with Level 3 distinction is currently under way as Google has already successfully driven cars in self-drive mode under restricted conditions (Litman, 2017) allowing human drivers to intervene when needed.

Google's self-driving car project, now called Waymo, represents cutting-edge technology toward Level 4 cars. Their Chrysler Pacifica Hybrid minivan is Waymo's "first vehicle built on a mass-production platform with a fully-integrated hardware suite . . . for the purpose of full autonomy" (Waymo, 2017).

Despite the rapid progress made toward autonomous vehicles, significant challenges still exist before Level 4 vehicles become commonplace. However, "once technological and regulatory issues have been resolved, up to 15 percent of new cars sold in 2030 could be fully autonomous" (McKensey and Company, 2016, p. 11).

CHALLENGES OF DEVELOPING AND IMPLEMENTING AUTONOMOUS TECHNOLOGIES

The most difficult challenge for expanding upon the existing technological developments with Level 4 and 5 vehicles and autonomous commercial drone deployment relates to creating regulatory frameworks "that will enable public and private entities to operate in full respect of safety, privacy and security concerns" (Floreano and Wood, 2015, p. 464).

In fact, only six states have passed laws allowing automakers to explore autonomous driving technology on public roads. Dr. Mary Cummings, professor in the Department of Mechanical Engineering and Materials Science at Duke University, recently asked North Carolina state legislators to develop an autonomous technology committee to get broader stakeholder buy-in for making plans in moving forward.

Safety Concerns versus Safety Benefits

According to the research and testing already conducted by Waymo and other carmakers such as Tesla, while autonomous vehicles provide more safety benefits than disadvantages, the issue of whether human controlled movement is safer than the prediction of movements of computer-controlled vehicles remains unclear.

> This is a problem because today, people rely upon cognitive intuitions about human behavior to avoid accidents with automobiles driven by other people. These same cognitive intuitions may not reliably apply when movement

decisions are made, not by people but by computer systems employing algorithms and sensor data (Surden and Williams, 2016, p. 180).

Dr. Cummings also addresses the safety challenges of refining sensory technology:

> The promise and potential benefits of driverless cars will be transformative . . . but significantly more research is needed in a range of areas, including sensor development, artificial intelligence and machine learning, the testing and evaluation of autonomous systems, and the legal, ethical, and public policy implications of driverless cars (Cummings, 2017, p. 37).

All research for the future of autonomous deployment indicates the technology for autonomous vehicles and drones remains stalled until the states take action to create legislation for the research and development of autonomous testing on public roads.

CHANGES ANTICIPATED IN AUTONOMOUS VEHICLES AND DRONES

Short Term

The issues regarding drones and autonomous vehicles will change dramatically as new technologies develop and become more mainstream. Public perception plays an essential role in how quickly new technology is accepted while public consumption directly promotes or inhibits demand.

In past years, important conversation revolved around the possible coming of these entities in the distant future. Now that the technology is here, the nation faces the enigma of finding best ways for implementing the new technology and integrating these vehicles with existing vehicles, as well as training the workforce on operations and repairs.

The short term includes predicted changes that will occur in the next three to five years. Discussions regarding the different levels of vehicle autonomy, ownership of the technology, human versus machine responsibility, safety, and legal liability are already surfacing as hot topics among professionals in the autonomous vehicle arena.

The recent Research Triangle Cleantech Cluster SMART series of meetings in North Carolina's Research Triangle Park are representative of the current conversations regarding infrastructure and implementation in some states and cities (RTCC, 2017). Waymo's recent allegations of trade secret theft of driverless car technology against Uber were referred to criminal court indicating a possible increase in tensions and lawsuits about ownership and patents (Mullin, 2017).

While this negative portrayal of self-driving vehicles in the media could damage the public's perception of self-driving vehicles, engineers, entrepreneurs, and leaders will continue to create advances. Local legislation may slow down progress in the short term causing some states to fall behind with adoption, implementation, and economic development as well.

Drones are evolving rapidly regarding technology, design, and use. "To most people a drone is one of two very different kinds of pilotless aircraft: a toy or a weapon" (The Economist Newspaper, 2017). However, a shift in perception will occur as the commercialization of drones become more common and the public sees drone technology applied to business and everyday use.

Drones already serve industries such as agriculture, cinematography, package delivery, construction and inspection; so, the obvious expectation for the next three to five years is an exponential increase in demand and usage.

Mid Term

There are three primary changes to watch for in the next five to ten years. Those changes revolve around the original technology, regulations for that technology, as well as the mergers of manufacturing and high-tech companies. As explained by Cummings, autonomous vehicles cannot yet accurately identify signs and objects on the roadway, thus continued improvements to the vehicle technology are vital (personal communication, May 19, 2017).

Other possible technologies in the next decade could involve changes in road regulations. For example, road signs of the future might be automated to transmit signals directly to the vehicles; thus, accommodating the new technology instead of trying to fit new vehicles into outdated road signs.

The aforementioned public perception of liability as well as consumption rates will indicate which level of autonomy is culturally acceptable in the next decade. As consumer rates increase in customer preference of the level of autonomy, it will require that the automotive sector works closely with high-tech companies to ensure all vehicles are functioning at the highest acceptable level with new capacities for each model.

Although drones and autonomous vehicles are distinctly different mechanisms, the next decade of research may connect the two for troubleshooting purposes including everything from mechanism design and technology to liability of programmer and operator. For example, one major problem with self-driving vehicles is the inability to recognize accurately signs and objects on roadways. However one of the major strengths of drone technology remains the multispectral view of the cameras that guide them.

Long Term

A short-term and mid-term progress bring about advances in drone and autonomous vehicle technologies, the long-term effects will be in the form of major culture shifts with regard to traffic rules and regulations, intellectual property, liability, high education and job training. Rapidly evolving technologies and designs will create the need to train employees quickly and potentially move job seekers away from a locked in two-year and four-year models of higher education.

Community colleges will be the institutions responsible for offering training of new skills for existing employees as well as training entry level positions specific to local companies. For jobs in this sector, increasing levels of proficiency concerning operating, programming, and repairing drones and autonomous vehicles may be more valuable than multiple degrees in higher education.

As large research universities primarily bear the responsibility of investigating and developing new drone and autonomous vehicle technologies and designs, as well as large scale testing, measuring the effects, and then publishing new findings, community colleges must prepare to serve an immediate, practical role (M. Cummings, personal communication, May 19, 2017).

IMPACT ON COMMUNITY COLLEGES

Community colleges are already known as the institutions of higher education that provide vocational and technical training; therefore, as the nation and the world prepare for a new technological revolution, community colleges are the obvious choice for providing short-term, technical training for the workforce that must use and repair new drone and autonomous vehicle technologies. In preparing for this shift, community colleges must consider the short-term, mid-term, and long-term implications.

Short Term

As companies introduce new technologies, employees will need immediate training that is also cost effective. In many cases, the technology introduced will be new for administrators, faculty and staff.

Some community colleges are already on board offering programs in drone piloting and engineering. For example, Monroe Community College in Michigan and Mohawk Valley Community College in Illinois partnered with an educational organization, SkyOp, and received recognition among the fifteen best drone training colleges for program offerings in Unmanned Aerial Systems (15 Best Drone Training Colleges website).

In the next three to five years, community colleges will need to gain momentum by growing these existing programs, adding new programs as needed, and acquiring new equipment and the latest technology. Achievement of these endeavors will result from building relationships and collaborating with industry for cost sharing opportunities.

Mid Term

In the next five to ten years, community colleges will face mounting challenges of finding resources including new equipment and new instructors as well as the technology necessary for training students in drone and autonomous vehicle programs. Increasing the speed of institutional change will also be a major mid-term challenge for these colleges.

Implementing new programs, updating existing programs, and acquiring equipment will take time. Approval from the accrediting body may delay the process. However, with the exponential speed of changing technology, community colleges must investigate methods to keep up with industry to remain relevant. Short-term, continuing education courses could be used to pave the way for more extensive programs to meet business and industry workforce needs.

Long Term

The long-term effects for community colleges will likely be a culture shift so immense that community colleges may face a bit of an identity crisis if they get behind the development of technology. Community colleges currently serve a broad range of students from literacy and basic skill to workforce development to university transfer degrees.

As the need for short-term credentials and technical workforce training increases, colleges likely may return to their vocational/technical roots, perhaps with redefined transfer divisions with a more practical mission as soft skills gain prominence.

One vision of the role of community colleges in the distant future of the autonomous vehicle arena is that of a transportation hub. If a company, such as Uber or Google, owns numerous self-driving cars and dispatches them to the consumer as needed, a physical site to store the vehicles will be necessary as well as vehicle maintenance and dispatch technologies. A community college could collaborate with the company to provide the service while training students on the job.

ANTICIPATED PROGRAMS AT COMMUNITY COLLEGES

Short Term

The Bureau of Labor Statistics identifies the twenty fastest growing occupations for the decade of 2014–2024, thirteen of which are healthcare occupations and industries (Bureau of Labor Statistics website, 2017). The remaining seven occupations include energy, finance, research and analytics related occupations.

If high school counselors, students, parents, and community college leaders use only the Bureau of Labor Statistics data table to identify the *Fastest Growing Occupations for 2014–2024* for the selection of future career paths and programming, the autonomous vehicle industry will not have an adequate number of prepared workers to move forward in the manner that this industry is advancing (Bureau of Labor Statistics: Fastest Growing Occupations website, 2017).

However, articles submitted to the Bureau of Labor Statistic's Monthly Labor Review reflect future trends in employment created by increased technology (Bureau of Labor Statistics: Monthly Labor Review website, 2017). Community colleges will need to add additional courses and programs to prepare workers for employment in future roles in the autonomous vehicle occupation market.

The autonomous vehicle industry will need workers who can expertly create specific parts for all types of autonomous vehicles. Associate degrees, diplomas, and certificates in Unmanned Aerial Vehicles (Drones) will be necessary programming for community college curricula and continuing education courses.

Possible programs are Associate Degrees in:

- Unmanned Aerial Systems Technology
- Unmanned Aerial Vehicle (Drone) Pilot Flight Training Certificate Program
- Federal Aviation Administration Drone Certification Course
- Drone Geographic Information Systems (GIS) and Mapping Program
- Drone Photography and Videography Certificate
- Drone Maintenance Diploma
- Law Enforcement Tactical Operations Certificate.

In addition, the colleges would be wise to consider entrepreneurial courses to assist students with starting drone-related, small businesses.

Mid Term

When considering autonomous vehicles as a mode of transportation, one has to take into account other academic and occupational disciplines which are critical to the communication, safety, and security of moving people or goods from one place to another. A White Paper examined Intelligent Transportation Systems (ITS), Connected Vehicles, Autonomous Vehicles, the changing workforce demographics, the education and training efforts of the ITS

Professional Capacity building (PCB) Program (Intelligent Transportation Systems, 2015).

One of the recommendations include the following:

> Utilize community colleges and technical schools to address training and education for those not requiring a university degree and to encourage/excite students to pursue university degrees in transportation. Community colleges and technical schools are a largely untapped resource that can be used to fill in gaps in technical training for those in professions not requiring a 4-year college degree such as maintenance technician, transportation communications specialists, etc. Community colleges can also act as a pipeline to attract and interest students to pursue degrees in transportation. In addition, they can provide individuals already in transportation and related professions to expand their knowledge as new technologies are implemented (Intelligent Transportation Systems, 2015, p. 9).

In the next five to ten years, community colleges need to carefully consider and plan for programming changes reflecting the anticipated advancements in technology. Associate degrees, diplomas, and certificates to consider include the following additions:

- An Associate Degree in Autonomous Vehicle System Technology, with an articulation agreement with universities.
- Engineering Apprenticeship programs in conjunction with employers in the service area to provide increased field training in autonomous vehicles.
- Associate Degrees in Transportation and Communications Engineering with an articulation agreement with universities should receive consideration.
- Additional certificate programs may be additives to the associate Degree in Engineering with a focus on software, communications, and design as related to the autonomous vehicle technology.

Community colleges should consider adding courses on Autonomous Vehicle Technology to the existing Engineering, Network, and Computer Technologies programs.

Long Term

In the next ten to twenty years, community colleges will be continuous, lifelong learning institutions. The partnerships with high schools, other community colleges, universities, and industry need to provide an environment whereby learners move seamlessly between the institutions and industry to obtain the training needed for their job duties. In ten to twenty years, community college academic programs would focus on the most current and anticipated future technology, innovation, and entrepreneurial occupational sectors. These programs may include:

- Autonomous Vehicle Fleet Management
- Autonomous Vehicle Systems Technology
- Autonomous Agricultural Systems Technology
- Autonomous Heavy Equipment
- Transport Technology
- Autonomous Construction Equipment Systems Technology

IMPACT ON COMMUNITY COLLEGE LEADERS

Short Term

Community college leaders of the future must possess the characteristics and qualities identified by the Aspen Institute and Achieving the Dream, which identified the skills and attributes needed by community college presidents to lead effective student success initiatives (Achieving the Dream website, 2017).

Community college leaders will effectively meet the demands of future programming if they demonstrate a deep commitment for student success, are willing to take calculated risks to establish new programs and initiatives, are skilled at developing plans and securing resources for moving forward with technology advances, can effectively manage change, embrace diversity, and lead teams through initiatives and culture shifts.

Community college leaders, in the next three to five years, should remain informed and proactive regarding the federal and state legislation on autonomous vehicles by often communicating with their local and state elected officials and keeping in touch with advances at the federal level.

Leaders involved with their college's local chamber of commerce, workforce development boards, and business and industry should participate in focused conversations regarding the impact autonomous vehicle legislation, regulations, and manufacturing will have on the workforce within the service area.

Hosting a Community Forum whereby informed legislators, technology experts, and manufacturing managers provide information and updates to the students, faculty, staff, and members of the community would facilitate interest, enthusiasm, and awareness of the potential of autonomous vehicles and the economic impact for the service area.

Providing the curriculum support and resources to advance efforts which educate students to design, manufacture, and maintain autonomous vehicles is the responsibility of community college leaders. The college's long-range strategic plan should include assessments, implementation actions, and annual evaluation efforts to assure that programming matches the technology advancements and workforce needs.

Mid Term

In addition to continuing to be proactive, involved, and informed, community college leaders, in the next five to ten years, need to evaluate the implementation of the early programming changes, delete obsolete programs, and merge in the additional programs. Using strategic planning, colleges must realign and reframe programming efforts to keep pace with the needs of the college's service area, technology, regulations, and manufacturing.

Engineering, Internet Technologies, Network and Connect Communications, Transportation, and Autonomous Vehicle Technologies will be mega programs within community colleges.

Leaders should anticipate the funding and resources needed to develop and maintain these programs, seek partnerships with high schools, other community colleges, universities, and business and industry. As community colleges educate people to advance with the technology, it changes the community as a whole.

Local firefighters, using drones, can track fire lines, the safety of their co-workers, and monitor the more remote areas. Farmers will use drones and autonomous vehicles in crop management activities such as reviewing crop growth progress, water and fertilizer needs, and aerial photography after storms to determine crop damage.

Long Term

In the long term, community college leaders will manage institutions that are vastly different from today's colleges. Community colleges will stand as the central hub of continuous, lifelong learning. The rapid advances in technology create a workforce environment that requires continual renewal of skills and knowledge.

Workers will retrain as fast as the technology advances. Students will move in, out, and through community colleges to obtain specific knowledge and skill sets that may only require a certificate level program. Many programs will be add-on courses or certificates to programs that currently exist.

In the next ten to twenty years, as technology changes, workers will use machines built before full automation, machines that were early-automated models, and machines of advanced technology, all in the same workday. Leading a community college during the mid-twenty-first century provides future presidents with an enormous leadership task. The preparation to do so begins now.

CONCLUSION

The most successful community college leaders in the future will consistently make decisions which are data-driven and relevant, supporting the college's mission, vision, and long-term strategic plan. Remaining flexible, responsive, a vital component of the community, and the economic driver of the service area, community colleges must serve as beacons and havens during times of crisis and change, but also in times of stability.

Futurist and subject-matter experts predict and provide focus, direction, and insight which community college leaders embrace. In the spirit of Hannibal Barca, the Carthaginian leader in 200 B.C., community college leaders must "find a way or make one" to launch programming strategies that provide the community with skilled, educated, and work-ready graduates who obtain life-sustaining wages (Biography website, 2015).

The individuals, their families, and the economic development of the community thrive only when leaders understand the exponential speed of the future as well as the past.

REFERENCES

Achieving the Dream website. (2017). http://achievingthedream.org/.

Aquino-Segarra, O. (2016). Drones: The need for more regulations. *Revista de Derecho Puertorrigueno, 55*(2), 335–353.

Biography website. (2015). https://www.biography.com/people/hannibal-9327767.

Bureau of Labor Statistics: Fastest Growing Occupations website. (2017). https://www.bls.gov/news.release/ecopro.t05.htm.

Bureau of Labor Statistics: Monthly Labor Review website. (2017). https://www.bls.gov/opub/mlr/.

Bureau of Labor Statistics website. (2017). https://www.bls.gov/.

Corrigan, F. (2017). How do drones work and what is drone technology. https://www.dronezon.com/learn-about-drones-quadcopters/what-is-drone-technology-or-how-does-drone-technology-work/.

Cummings, M. (2017). The brave new world of driverless cars: The need for interdisciplinary research and workforce development. *TR News,* 34–37. https://hal.pratt.duke.edu/sites/hal.pratt.duke.edu/files/u24/TRN_308_Cummings_%20pp34-37%20web.pdf.

Cummings, M. (2015). What to do about drones. http://www.cnn.com/2015/01/29/opinion/cummings-drone-policies/index.html.

DeAngelis, J. (2016, June 15). Planning for the autonomous vehicle revolution [Blog post]. https://www.planning.org/blog/blogpost/9105024/.

Defense Advanced Research Projects Agency (DARPA) website. (n.d.). https://www.darpa.mil/about-us/about-darpa.

Defense Advanced Research Projects Agency (DARPA) website. (n.d.). https://www.darpa.mil/work-with-us/for-universities.

Floreano, D., & Wood, R. J. (2015, May 28). Science, technology and the future of small autonomous drones. *Nature, 521*(7553), 460–466. http://dx.doi.org/10.1038/nature14542.

Frey, T. (2015). 101 endangered jobs by 2030. *Journal of Environmental Health, 77*(9), 40–42.

Litman, T. (2017). *Autonomous vehicle implementation predictions: Implications for transport planning* [White paper]. http://www.vtpi.org/avip.pdf.

McKensey & Company. (2016). *Automotive revolution- perspective towards 2030: How the convergence of disruptive technology-driven trends could transform the auto industry* [White paper]. http://www.mckinsey.com/search?q=automotive%20revolution%20%E2%80%93%20perspective%20towards%202030.

Mullin, J. (2017). Judge refers Waymo v. Uber lawsuit to criminal investigators. https://arstechnica.com/tech-policy/2017/05/judge-uber-cant-push-waymo-lawsuit-into-arbitration.

Price, H. (2017). Fact sheet - FAA forecasts - fiscal years 2016-37. https://www.faa.gov/news/fact_sheets/news_story.cfm?newsId=21514.

Research Triangle Cleantech Cluster. (2017). Transformation through Collaboration. https://d3n8a8pro7vhmx.cloudfront.net/rtcc/pages/44/attachments/original/1495223157/SMART_Series_Autonomous_Vehicle_Presentations_5.19.2017.pdf?1495223157.

SAE International. (2016, September 22). *U. S. Department of Transportation's new policy on automated vehicles adopts SAE International's levels of automation for defining driving automation in on-road motor vehicles* [Press release]. https://www.sae.org/news/3544/.

Self-Driving Coalition for Safer Streets. (2017). Safety, disability, & mobility advocates partner with self-driving coalition for safer streets. http://www.selfdrivingcoalition.org/newsroom/press-releases/safety-disability-mobility-advocates-partner-with-self-driving-coalition-for-safer-streets.

Surden, H., & Williams, M. (2016). Technological opacity, predictability, and self-driving cars. *Cardozo Law Review, 38*(1), 121–181.

Successful Student website. (n.d.). 15 best drone training colleges. http://successful-student.org/15-best-drone-training-colleges/.

The Aspen Institute website. (2017). https://www.aspeninstitute.org/.

The Economist Newspaper. (2017). A new type of drone, neither military nor civilian, is emerging. http://www.economist.com/blogs/graphicdetail/2017/06/daily-chart-6.

U.S. Bureau of Labor Statistics. (2015). *Employment projections: 2014-24 summary* (USDL-15-2327). Washington, DC: Government Printing Office.

University Programs in Intelligent Transportation Systems (ITS): The Evolving Transportation Engineering Discipline. (2015). https://www.pcb.its.dot.gov/documents/whitepaper_university_pgms_in_ITS.aspx.

Waymo. (2017). Journey. https://waymo.com/journey/.

Chapter 5

The Internet of Things

Darrel W. Staat

"Marshall McLuhan's Global Village has arrived and the digital age is flourishing."

—Samuel Greengard

In less than twenty years the Internet grew from an idea that seemed almost science-fiction to a reality that affects just about everything. The Internet has had a tremendous impact on business, politics, and personal lives by bringing the entire world into the personal computer and cell phone.

Back in the early 1990s, a speaker came to a Rotary Club meeting in Maine to talk about the effect the Internet might have on businesses in the future. He was in his early twenties speaking to a group of mostly men whose average age was about sixty years old. The speaker painted a picture of how businesses would use the Internet to sell their products, how retail would change to purchases made over cyberspace, and how personal lives would be changed significantly.

He envisioned everything from buying clothing to cars from home computers. He said that everyone needed to understand the power of this new digital technology. He was excited and the audience listened intently to gain some insight into the topic.

However, on the way out of the meeting many of the members were not convinced. Almost no one took him seriously. They thought the speaker was talking science-fiction. They thought things were going to stay pretty much as they were and the Internet was most likely just a fad that might be useful to a university. They were wrong.

Within one year almost every one of those business leaders in the Rotary Club had a website and was beginning to understand the immense possibilities the Internet held for the success of their businesses. Today the Internet is almost *passé*. It is an infrastructure that is taken for granted like electricity in homes or highways for travel. It has invaded our homes, our lives, our businesses. Children assume it always existed, because at least in their lifetimes, it has.

INVASION OF THE INTERNET OF THINGS

Now, some tweny years later, just as the Internet is accepted as normal, something new has quietly slipped onto the scene almost without notice, the Internet of Things (IoT). Whereas in the past individuals have been somewhat knowledgeable of the new technologies, the IoT is moving into our work and lives without asking permission.

Samuel Greengard (2015) sees the IoT as "a shockwave coming at us that is just beginning to be felt" (p. xii). Michael Miller (2015) states, "the Internet of things is coming. It is going to be big. It is going to be important. It is going to impact your life" (p. 5).

It almost sounds like a repetition of the Rotary Club meeting back in the early 1990s when members heard about the Internet and wanted to ignore it. Now, well over twenty years later, another new technology has appeared upon the scene. Should it be ignored, laughed at, or taken seriously?

Current Status

At present, the IoT provides information to consumers. For example, the heating and cooling of a home is controlled by means of a thermostat. It is a sensor that when set attains the temperature desired in the house. Late-model automobiles inform the driver when they need maintenance. Amazon's Echo allows an individual to control many electronic devices in the home. However, in the near future the Internet of things will spread a much wider net.

The Internet of things can connect:

- Home electronic devices, such as smart televisions and streaming media servers
- Medical devices such as pacemakers and heart monitoring implants
- Home appliances, such as smart refrigerators, ovens, and laundry machines
- Automobiles, including self-driving cars
- Airplanes large and small, from commercial airliners to self-flying drones
- Home automation devices, such as thermostats, smoke detectors, and alarm systems
- Homes, towns, cities, and nations, just about everything that can be monitored and controlled (Miller, 2015, p. 8)

Soon the IOT will literally be everywhere, in everything. What can be expected when the IoT goes full bore?

The Gartner research firm estimates the IOT will connect close to 26 billion devices by 2020. Competing research firm Allied Business Intelligence (ABI) research says the number will be more than 30 billion. Tech powerhouse CISCO prophesies 50 billion devices in the same timeframe; Nelson Research says 100 billion devices; Intel says 200 billion; International Data Corporation (IDC) says 212 billion (Miller, 2015, p. 12).

According to these predictors, somewhere between 26 billion and 212 billion devices are to be connected through the Internet of Things by 2020. That will develop largely with little input or critique from individuals, governments, or businesses.

As the numbers increase, three things will take place; first, the data will be collected by sensors; second, the collected data will be stored in the cloud, and third it will be analyzed (Miller, 2015). The big questions are, who will analyze the data and for what purpose?

The need for analysis will most likely generate new jobs to develop, run, and analyze the data. New algorithms will be developed to assist in the processing. Ultimately, business executives will make decisions based on the data analysis. In other words, the IoT will morph current data analysis completed by the business to an entirely new digital level of competence, efficiency, and effectiveness.

The IoT will be accepted when people see value in the technologies that help them live safer, more comfortable, and more successful lives. There will always be the possibility of a reaction against the IoT, but since the process will be incremental, the methodology will be in place before most individuals are even aware of it.

The key trends driving this [IoT] technology development are:

- Miniaturization: electronic devices have become smaller and more powerful, driven by Moore's Law, but also by improvements in electrical power management.
- Affordability: the cost of electronic components and networks have been consistently going down, also driven by Moore's Law to a large extent.
- Dewireization: more and more things are becoming wireless, which means they can be located anywhere [through the use of Radio Frequency Identification (RFID)]. The growing ubiquity of cellular and Wi-Fi networks has driven this trend (Kellemereit et al., 2013, p. 14).

At the moment, these sensors report to individuals as owners; however, in the very near future, they will also report to the manufacturer, the retail business, and, more significantly, to each other. The consumer will benefit directly, but so will the manufacturers and businesses. As time goes by, the world will become totally interconnected through the Internet of Things.

Velocity of IoT Growth

The IoT phenomenon is not coming in a flash or with great fanfare; rather it is developing in the background almost without much awareness. The possibilities for good and bad uses of the IoT are self-evident. How positive or negative will it be? Time will tell, but since the world is rapidly changing, it may not be long before the impact is felt.

The worst-case scenario would cause individuals to lose control over everyday activities now seen as normal, which many may not appreciate. A smart refrigerator, which would know when the food levels are low and could contact the local grocer for replacements that would be delivered to the door, may not seem like a good idea if the individuals involved were interested in doing their own shopping. Best-case scenario would see an increase in helpful activities ranging from a car that drives itself to appliances that contact the repairman when something goes wrong.

Short Term

In the near future, IoT sensors will appear in cars, appliances, cell phones, clothing, medical devices, and more. Most likely the addition of sensors will be seen as aids to making life easier and more efficient.

Mid Term

In five–ten years the IoT technology will expand to the point where some objects will not only talk to the consumer, but will communicate directly to the manufacturers, businesses, and each other. Autonomous cars will have sensors that can communicate with other autonomous cars on the highway to keep accidents from occurring or allowing a set of autonomous vehicles to follow each other more closely than normal, which will allow them to arrive at the destination in less time.

Long Term

In twenty years autonomous cars will be available and used by most everyone. Smart homes will be available to those who are interested. At first, smart homes will be purchased by the wealthy, but as the costs come down they will become available in all house construction. Appliances and clothing will contain sensors, even if the consumer does not find them to their benefit. Manufacturers and retail businesses will receive considerable data from the sensors that will be useful to them for future construction and sales.

Michael Miller (2015) states, "We are talking about a decade or several decades before the majority of items and systems are compatible and connected to IoT" (p. 12). Most likely the inclusion of sensors for IoT will come sooner rather than later as there is, at present, nothing to stop them and they appear to be of some value to the consumer and beyond.

IMPACT ON COMMUNITY COLLEGES

If, as expected, the IoT makes considerable progress in becoming a normal part of everyday life and work, what effect does that have on community colleges and their leaders?

Short Term

Community college leaders need to become aware of the IoT phenomenon. They need to determine if the IoT is accepted by their constituents: the business community, students, and the residents of the college service area. If IoT is not accepted, leaders can continue business as usual, at least for the time being. Since IoT is an exponential phenomenon, it is currently developing along the blade in the hockey stick metaphor. When IoT hits the upswing at the shaft, leaders will have to be prepared to act, if they have not taken steps previously.

On the other hand, if the IoT is accepted by those concerned, community college leaders will need to immediately get prepared for change. They do not want to react as the Rotary Club members referenced earlier did, dismissing the Internet as something that might affect them some time in the future, if ever. To be forewarned is to be forearmed.

They need to be aware and prepared to move swiftly in new directions required by the IoT technology. If IoT expands as rapidly as the Internet did, community college leaders cannot be caught flat-footed. They must be preparing for the opportunities that will be created by IoT.

Students may be the most informed and best prepared for the IoT changes, just as was evident of their acceptance of the Internet in the early 1990s. Simultaneously, as the business community members change their operations to include IoT, they will expect that the community colleges, which are training their workforces, are up to date on how that technology is affecting their businesses and what needs to be done to train their workforce.

Mid Term

If technological change is hard to keep up in the present, staying abreast with it in the future may be exponentially more difficult. New programs of study will be needed in rapid fashion. Programs in entrepreneurial education will become critical as more individuals attempt to start new digital businesses. Training in data analytics will become necessary.

A general program in the IoT will be needed by the business community, health organizations, and individual members of the community. The program needs may be met initially through short courses in Continuing Education. Faculty will specific skill sets may have to be hired or existing faculty may need to be trained to meet new business and health care needs.

Long Term

The successful community college leader in the future will be one who is able to foresee the changes coming, assess what is needed in terms of equipment, training and education, and provide the development needed for the faculty to meet the needs that continually and exponentially develop.

Urban and suburban community colleges will most likely see rapid, almost unpredictable changes in program offerings, while rural institutions may find that change is more gradual, but it will arrive. Community colleges have for decades prided themselves on the fact that they can turn on a dime to meet the training needs of business and industry. The next ten to twenty years will put that ability to the extreme test. As exponential change replaces linear development, the effect on community colleges will be significant beyond anything experienced in the past.

CONCLUSION

The Internet of Things is just one of a number of technological changes facing the community college in the twenty-first century. One needs to anticipate that those technologies will intertwine and build on each other to create even more unforeseen situations. Community colleges will need to constantly research the technology in order to expand their grand tradition of providing educational and training support to their students, the business community, local economic development and the community in general.

REFERENCES

Greengard, Samuel. (2015). *The internet of things*. Cambridge, MA: MIT Press, Essential Knowledge Series.

Kellmereit, Daniel, & Obodovski, Daniel. (2013). *The silent intelligence: The internet of things*. San Francisco, CA: DnD Ventures.

Miller, Michael. (2015). *The internet of things: How smart TVs, smart cars, smart homes, and smart cities are changing the world*. Indianapolis, IN: Que Publishing.

Pew Research Center. (2014). *The internet of things will thrive by 2025*. http://www.Pewinternet.org/2014/05/14/internet-of-things/.

Chapter 6

Genome Development: Medical

Melodie Hunnicutt, Renie Johnston, and John "Scott" Stauble Jr.

"In the middle of every difficulty lies opportunity."

—Thomas Edison

Few technological advances have the power to change the very fabric of society like advances in genomics. Genomics, or the study of DNA and its functions, is at the core of every living organism on the planet.

The power of grasping the details of the DNA function and being able to modify those functions has been hailed as the Holy Grail for improving human life, from medical advances to ending hunger. Like most technologies, the study of genomics jumps forward in exponential leaps that have life-changing effects on humanity and profound implications for community colleges.

A BRIEF HISTORY OF GENOMICS

In 1953, James Watson and Francis Crick, with the help of Rosalind Franklin, described the structure of DNA for the first time (US Department of Energy [US DoE], 2008). With the knowledge of DNA structure revealed, scientists launched the field of genomics to answer the question of how this molecule at the center of every cell functioned to run that cell and thus the entire organism.

From the 1950s to 1980s, many key studies were done that further revealed the function of DNA in creating proteins and how information was stored in the structure of DNA (US DoE, 2008). The next big step forward in genomics, however, came in 1990 with the commencement of the Human Genome Project (HGP).

With the ambitious goal of sequencing all three billion letters of the human genome, the Human Genome Project (HGP) promised to fundamentally change our understanding of humanity. The HGP was completed in 2003, making the full genome of not only humans available, but technologies developed during completion of the project meant that the genome of all species could now be sequenced in a matter of days or weeks, rather than years.

With a fundamental knowledge of the actual sequence of base pairs in the DNA of numerous organisms, scientists began the second leap forward in genomics. Knowing the sequence of letters in the DNA strand meant that scientists could find ways to change those letters.

Through numerous methods developed in the 2000s and early 2010s, scientists could change DNA structures to produce hardier crop species to alleviate hunger, to assist in the treatment of disease, and to develop bacteria that can clean up toxic waste, among numerous other developments (US DoE, 2008).

The drive to alter DNA in hopes of providing a benefit for humanity has now led to a third leap in genomics research, the discovery of Clustered Regularity Interspaced Short Palindromic Repeats (CRISPR) systems in bacteria, which make altering DNA as easy as it is to sequence DNA now. In the following sections, the use of genomics and genetic engineering to alter DNA will be explored.

The first topic will discuss the development of CRISPR and its effects on basic scientific research, including how community colleges will need to respond to changing genomic technologies as the colleges train research assistants through biotechnology programs.

The second topic will discuss how new genetic technologies are impacting the field of medicine and how those changes might lead to community colleges needing to alter their approach to training healthcare professionals. Chapter seven will focus on how genomics is altering the field of agriculture and how such changes might affect programmatic and curricular content in community colleges in the future.

CURRENT TRENDS IN GENOMICS: CRISPR REVOLUTION

In 2012, Emmanuelle Charpentier and Jennifer Doudna published a paper describing the transformative power of a new system of DNA editing discovered in bacteria, the CRISPR-Cas9 system (Sanders, 2017). CRISPR-Cas9 made altering the sequence of a DNA strand faster and more accurate, allowing for targeted changes to be made to the DNA in a way that few other genomic technologies could accomplish.

In 2013, using the work of Charpentier and Doudna, the first researchers reported that they had used the CRISPR-Cas9 system to alter a copy of the human genome at a site of the researchers' choosing (Ledford, 2016; Zimmer, 2016). From that point until today, genomics has been advancing by leaps and bounds beginning at the level of basic biological research.

Understanding CRISPR

CRISPR is an acronym for "clustered regularly interspaced palindromic repeats" (Doudna and Charpentier, 2014, p. 1). The name refers to specific sequences of DNA discovered in bacteria by scientists in 1987 (Hau, Lander, and Zhang, 2014). These DNA sequences are unique in that while finding base pair repeats in a strand of DNA is not abnormal, they are usually linked directly together.

In the case of CRISPR, however, the palindromic repeats are "interspaced," meaning that there were other DNA sequences separating the repeated segments. According to Hau, Lander and Zhang (2014), this curious arrangement of repeats stimulated much speculation, but no purpose for these special portions of DNA was discovered until the early 2000s.

Doudna and Chapentier (2014) report that in 2005, it was discovered that the spacing sequences in CRISPR, that is, the sequences of DNA that separated the repeating sequences, were derived primarily from viral DNA. In other words, small pieces of viral DNA were being inserted into the bacterial DNA sandwiched between repeating segments.

Finally, in 2007, it was found that these CRISPR segments of DNA acted as an immune system of sorts for bacterial cells. When a bacterium was infected by a virus, it would insert a small portion of that virus' DNA into its own DNA in the form of the CRISPR sequences.

The next time that same virus infects that bacterium, the bacterium can use the DNA sequence stored in the CRISPR repeats to recognize that virus and then destroy the viral DNA before it has the opportunity to infect and destroy the cell. At its core, the CRISPR system is a kind of immune system for bacterial cells (Butler and Tector, 2017; Doudna and Charpentier, 2014; Hau, Lander, and Zhang, 2014).

While stored viral DNA sequences in the CRISPR system allowed for the recognition of viral DNA, it is actually another enzyme, known as Cas9, which allows for the destruction of new invading viral DNA (Doudna and Charpentier, 2014; Hau, Lander, and Zhang, 2014).

At this point, the scientific community had a collective thought. If Cas9 can make cuts in the DNA strands by being guided by RNA to a specific location in the DNA to make that cut, could artificially made RNA, designed to cut a sequence of a scientist's choosing, also guide Cas9 to make a targeted cut?

As it turned out, the answer to the question was positive, and the genomic science has not looked back since. Scientists had already discovered ways to alter DNA structure and function, but they were costly, slow, and unreliable processes. The newly discovered CRISPR-Cas9 system, as it is now called, was just the opposite. It was quick, relatively inexpensive, and offered "the ability to target and study particular DNA sequences in the vast expanse of a genome" (Ledford, 2016, p. 157).

With the basics of CRISPR-Cas9 described, scientists then turned to applying this new technology to numerous fields. The field that is currently most affected by the development of CRISPR-Cas9 systems is basic biological research (K. Doxzen, Innovative Genomics Institute, personal communication, June 25, 2017).

Future of Basic Research with CRISPR

Before any major scientific breakthrough can have a true effect on society that breakthrough must find the avenues through which it can be applied successfully and safely. At the core of finding those avenues is basic research. CRISPR-Cas9 genomic technology is no exception in that its largest impact to date is in the realm of basic research. The power and the limitations of CRISPR-Cas9 must be explored in order to know exactly how this new advance can be applied.

CRISPR-Cas9 systems have been applied in various ways to improve basic scientific research. For example, it was soon discovered that the Cas9 enzyme, which normally cuts DNA when it binds, could be disabled. Instead of cutting the DNA, the Cas9 enzyme would bind to the specific part of DNA that the provided RNA template led it to, but would then do nothing.

As Ledford (2016) describes, this means that the segment of DNA that the Cas9 enzyme was bound to had been effectively disabled. This technique allows genes within an organism's DNA to be disabled without actually altering the DNA strand itself (Ledford, 2016). By now being able to turn genes on and off at will, a more concerted effort is being undertaken to describe the function of numerous genes whose functions were unknown in the past. The disabled CRISPR-Cas9 also makes it possible for numerous genes to be turned off or on at once, allowing for studies on the interaction between genes and inter genomic effects (Ledford, 2016).

Another major area of genomic research is epigenetics, which studies the "constellation of chemical compounds tacked onto DNA" and how those chemical compounds affect DNA function (Ledford, 2016, p. 157). Along with disabling Cas9, scientists further discovered that they could attach epigenetic elements to the disabled Cas9 protein, leading to upregulations or downregulations of gene expression in the area of the Cas9 binding. A similar technique also allows genes to be turned off and on with the use of light by binding a light-sensitive protein to Cas9, providing even more tightly regulated control to the future research studies (Ledford, 2016).

CRISPR-Cas9 systems are also being employed to create genetically engineered animals and plants for a variety of purposes. For example, by creating animals that more closely model human diseases, such as cancer and diabetes, the efficacy of drug trials to treat these diseases can be greatly improved (Smith, 2017).

Further, current CRISPR-Cas9 studies are being done on pigs to remove elements from their cells that the human immune system would naturally attack, allowing for the possible use of pig organs for human transplant in the future, a major boon to millions of people on organ donor waiting lists (Butler and Tector, 2017).

With these and numerous other CRISPR-Cas9 applications in the works, Travis (2015) summarizes the power of this new system, saying "[it is] only slightly hyperbolic to say that if scientists can dream of a genetic manipulation, CRISPR can now make it happen" (p. 1457).

IMPACT ON THE COMMUNITY COLLEGE

As CRISPR-Cas9 systems become more predominant in the world of biological research, especially in the basic sciences, industries are going to expect that students will be trained in the usage of these technologies before they begin their employment. It is not unfair to say that CRISPR technology is going to become more ubiquitous not only in industry but in basic science laboratories in the future.

According to one report, CRISPR-Cas9 technology has become so inexpensive that $150 kits can be purchased to perform CRISPR-Cas9 experiments in the privacy of individual homes (Yu, 2017). Therefore, it will be expected that CRISPR-Cas9 will be taught to students in community colleges as well.

Short Term

Given that some of the largest changes in industry are occurring in basic science, it seems logical that likely changes in the next three to five years will be focused in the field of biotechnology. To determine what effects CRISPR-Cas9 technology will have in the training of biotechnology students, six community college biotechnology instructors were consulted about their thoughts on CRISPR-Cas9 and the effects this new technology might have on their programs in the future.

Currently, biotechnology programs at the community college level are focused on cell culture, bioinformatics, and manipulating DNA through other methods besides CRISPR-Cas9 (L. A. Holston, Johnston Community College, personal communication, June 27, 2017; M. Sabaoun, Alamance Community College, personal communication, June 22, 2017; A. Waddell, Southwest Tennessee Community College, personal communication, June 23, 2017).

The following sections will discuss how community college biotechnology programs may change in the future in response to the CRISPR-Cas9 revolution and how funding may need to change as a result.

Changes in program offerings. In discussions with biotechnology faculty at community colleges, it was clear that nearly all community college biotechnology programs were teaching CRISPR-Cas9 technology to some degree. Most had integrated CRISPR-Cas9 information into their lectures (L. Fletcher, Austin Community College, personal communication, June 23, 2017; L. A. Holston, Johnston Community College, personal communication, June 27, 2017; D. Kovarik, Shoreline Community College, personal communication, June 22, 2017; E. Steiner, Niagara Community College, personal communication, June 25, 2017).

One had gone as far as to start developing lab techniques for CRISPR-Cas9 use (M. Sabaun, Alamance Community College, personal communication, June 22, 2017). It is obvious that biotechnology instructors at community colleges have thought deeply about the impact that CRISPR-Cas9 is likely to have on their programs, including how their programs may need to change in the near and long-term futures.

L. Fletcher (personal communication, June 23, 2017) and A. Waddell (Southwest Tennessee Community College, personal communication, June 23, 2017) stressed the importance of having a strong program advisory board with members from biotechnology companies in the region the community college serves. These advisory boards make certain that the technology being taught at the community college is up to date with the technology needed in industry.

While CRISPR-Cas9 is still being developed, in the next three to five years, it is likely that community colleges will need to focus on training students in the areas of bioinformatics and tissue culture, as these are areas that many companies are currently moving into (L. Fletcher, personal communication, June 23, 2017; M. Sabaoun, personal communication, June 22, 2017; E. Steiner, personal communication, June 25, 2017).

Mid Term

In the next ten to twenty years, however, things begin to get less clear in terms of direction. As Doxzen states, "scientists [do not] often like to speculate about things too far in the future because often times [they] will be wrong" (personal communication, June 25, 2017). Scientists are entirely unclear about where this new technology will lead, and thus community college biotechnology instructors are equally unclear of the future of their programs.

However, Holston (personal communication, June 27, 2017) had some insight about the future structure of biotechnology programs. In the next ten to twenty years, she predicts that community colleges may be less focused on degrees and more focused on "short-term, intensive certifications that pair well with advanced degrees" (L. Holston, personal communication, June 27, 2017).

As CRISPR-Cas9 ushers in a new wave of genomic advances, it may become more important for community colleges to provide training for individuals with advanced degrees than to provide *de novo* instruction in those new technologies.

Long Term

It is possible that as technology advances, community colleges will become the place where people already working in the field of basic scientific research turn to for training in the newest technologies. These new certifications can be a part of an overall curriculum culminating in an Applied Associate Degree in Biotechnology, but should also be able to be offered as individual certificates for those who only need to train or to review new developments in one area.

Holston suggests that technical writing, quality management, aseptic techniques, robotics in biotechnology, the basics of CRISPR-Cas9, and other technique-based certificates could be developed to meet the needs of the ever-evolving biotechnology industry (personal communication, June 27, 2017).

THE CRISPR REVOLUTION IN PERSONAL MEDICINE

Riding the wave of CRISPR technology and its myriad of promising future pathways will be a quest that community colleges will be tasked with keeping pace with. Yet CRISPR is not the only tool that will need monitoring. If this tool is to be as useful as it promises to be, it will need support from other areas of science, particularly continuing biotechnological instrumentation and treatment protocol advancement.

From Bacteria to Tool

This technology that has come from the lowly bacteria has been used for billions of years to protect other bacteria and archaea by providing adaptive immunity to invasive genetic elements. Dr. Rodolphe Barrangou of North Carolina State University's CRISPR lab explains: "It is the DNA-driven equivalent of our own adaptive immune system, just on a single cell level rather than an organismal level. This is what CRISPR Cas9 systems are in nature at their most basic level" (personal communication, July 13, 2017).

Scientists have discovered how to use this system to produce molecular enzymatic machines. These machines are the Cas9 portion of the systems. These are the genome editing machines that are being used to create a revolution in biology. Dr. Barrangou said, "The irony is there is no CRISPR in CRISPR; it is the machine derived from CRISPR that does the editing" (personal communication, July 13, 2017). The Cas9 machine is now being produced artificially and we no longer need CRISPR to produce it.

What can CRISPR do currently?

This technology can be used to repair genetic mutations. Many diseases are genetic in nature. Some of them are simple mutations that are caused by a single out of place nitrogenous base. Others are very complicated and involve multiple genes and other machinery that is associated with the DNA system.

CRISPR technology will be used to correct the simpler defects first. The more deadly and widespread the disease, the more attention it will get from the research labs. Some applications can be widely used without having to be individualized because they will be treating genetic diseases that are well-documented. Other applications will require a more personal approach and have to be tailored to the patient (R. Barrangou, personal communication, July 14, 2017).

Short Term

In the next five years, CRISPR technology will be in clinical trials. A clinical trial is a research study to determine if the treatment will be safe and effective for humans. It is projected that this will begin in 2018. Each clinical trial is different, and trials must progress through various phases. During the last phases of these trials, "CRISPR technology will be used to cure or alter a faulty DNA sequence in a human patient, not a cell, not an animal, but a human. This is the biggest thing - in effect drug development" (R. Barrangou, personal communication, July 14, 2017).

Mid Term

Within the next ten years, the results of CRISPR technology will be in pharmacies, as well as in hospitals. "The applications will be sold in the market to any patient who needs it anywhere. We will learn to produce cures for liver, blood, and eye diseases and then deliver the cure to the organ. It will eradicate the problem, in every single cell, every single time" (R. Barrangou, personal communication, July 14, 2017).

The cure for all human genetically-derived diseases will not be coming in five, 10 or even 20 years. Many diseases are more complex, like cancer, and are caused by many mutations and involve so many genes. Treating cancer will increase the level of complexity greatly because it affects too many tissues that have a network of interaction between different cell types. . . . This will be one of the challenges that will be tackled, how to get the therapy into more cells (R. Barrangou, personal communication, July 14, 2017).

Long Term

In twenty years, there will have been much information released to the public about the therapies that have resulted from the CRISPR phenomenon. Yet there will always be a faction of the human population that is reluctant to face change.

There will be people who are not willing to participate in these new technologies. Who will say, don't cure my cancer, muscular dystrophy, HIV, or sickle cell anemia. This will be a case for natural selection. Just as vaccination has saved multiple orders in the magnitude of people more than it has inured (R. Barrangou, personal communication, July 14, 2017).

These people will still need to be treated, and other technologies will also be advancing during this time. Perhaps a parallel to the CRISPR technology will be discovered in a more conventional treatment pathway, but it will not likely be as explosively influential as the CRISPR technologies.

Moore's Law months has been applied to the CRISPR technology revolution. Just considering publications, citations, and patented positions, Dr. Barrangou stated,

When I began with CRISPR in 2004, there were approximately one hundred papers published total. Now the numbers are on the track to have 4,000 CRISPR studies published this year. If you look at shipment numbers of orders for CRISPR plasmids at the 2016 pace, 24,000 shipments were made in the form of a product called Addgene. This works out to 500 shipments a day. Every hour, 16 new labs will be working the CRISPR system technology. Those shipments include 60 countries. These numbers show the democratization of the CRISPR technology, and it is just beginning (R. Barrangou, personal communication, July 14, 2017).

ROLE OF THE HUMAN GENOME PROJECT IN CRISPR

This is not a tool that can operate without the contributions of other technologies. The Human Genome Project (HGP) helped to spur interest in the general public for the scientific endeavors that are rapidly changing current perspectives in medicine. The tools that made HGP possible have not been left in the tool box to rust. They have been improved, and their existence has inspired other tools and procedures to be discovered.

Advancements in this field feed off each subsequent success or failure. To be able to treat the malfunctioning portions of DNA, the locations first have to be located and mapped. In some cases, computers have been added to the mix to literally program the synthesis of DNA molecules.

The ability to design and manufacture synthetic DNA has opened tremendous possibilities in genomic research, such as biomolecular computing, metabolic engineering and reconstruction and exploration of natural cell biology. These new fields commonly require the design of new genetically encoded systems (Galdzicki et al., 2013).

Many in the general public think that the HGP has completed a comprehensive listing of all the DNA in the human genome. It does not. There is some ambiguity about how much is not completed. The HGP project has finished sequencing 99 percent of the human gene-containing regions (Nation Institutes of Health, 2003). This project allowed scientists to have a guide or map to use when attempting to locate the genes they were looking for.

One of the next steps is to complete the one percent that is not mapped. There is much more to the human genome than the gene-containing regions. These non-gene regions have a name that is not entirely true; they are called Junk-DNA.

In science, the more one knows, the more one learns what one does not know, is a very accurate statement. Junk-DNA was not mapped in the HGP due to the limitations of the technology. Some of these limitations have been overcome, and others will soon be conquered as well. There will soon be even more for CRISPR technology to do.

The Promise of CRISPR

Dr. Barrangou's dream is for CRISPR to be an "opportunity for the grand public to appreciate science for what it is and scientists for who they are and technology for what it does" (personal communication, July 14, 2017). Scientists are problem solvers. They develop tools and use them to cure diseases and address ambitious challenges, such as finding a cure for HIV, cancer and the worldwide food shortage with the need to feed one billion more people by 2050. CRISPR will help with those tasks. In Dr. Barrangou's words,

> CRISPR has the ability to be a disruptive technology that will enable the scientific illiterate . . . to appreciate how science and technology can solve problems and make an impact that can benefit mankind. CRISPR will be the best example of how technology can help humankind in medicine, food, agriculture, breeding, antimicrobials, antibiotics, and microbiology" (R. Barrangou, personal communication, July 14, 2017).

CRISPR'S INFLUENCE ON COMMUNITY COLLEGES

Short Term

The CRISPR technology is already making it into high school textbooks. Students will be coming to colleges and universities, including community colleges already knowing the basics concerning CRISPR technology as a tool whose general use is to cut and edit DNA. The fields that will be most affected by CRISPR technology will be genetics, biology, biochemistry, and microbiology, essentially the biological fields.

Mid Term

These fields will need to add a chapter to their books and as well as time in the classroom to inform students about CRISPR. As the CRISPR technology is used to produce genetic therapies and other treatments, healthcare programs will need to adapt to accommodate training in these treatments as well.

Long Term

Twenty years out, there may even be genetic clinics that will need several different types of healthcare workers, just as the dental field does today. The community colleges will be there to provide those trained workers for these clinics, as well as hospitals and other outpatient medical providers. CRISPR technology is an illustration of the need to stay current.

> Keep your curriculum tweaked to stay current. To use an analogy, you don't need to rebuild the building, only renovate it, to accommodate the new tasks that will be required. The high schools, colleges, and universities will be tasked with educating the masses about this tool (R. Barrangou, personal communication, July 14, 2017).

REFERENCES

Butler, J. R., & Tector, A. J. (2017). CRISPR genome-editing: A medical revolution. *The Journal of Thoracic and Cardiovascular Surgery, 153*(2), 488–491. doi:10.1016/j.jtcvs.2016.08.067.

Doudna, J. A., & Charpentier, E. (2014). The new frontier of genome engineering with CRISPR-Cas9. *Science, 346*(6213), 1–9. doi:10.1126/science.1258096.

Galdzicki, M. (2013, June 21). The Synthetic Biology Open Language (SBOL) provides a community standard for communicating designs in synthetic biology. *Nature America.* https://eds.b.ebscohost.com.portnoy.wingate.edu/eds/pdfviewer/pdfviewer?vid=36&sid=1565c392-2005-47b6-b830-622696aba49f%40session mgr4006.

Hau, P. D., Lander, E. S., & Zhang, F. (2014). Development and applications of CRISPR-Cas9 for genome engineering. *Cell, 157*, 1262–1278. doi:10.1016/j.cell.2014.05.010.

Ledford, H. (2016). Riding the CRISPR wave: Biologists are embracing the power of gene-editing tools to explore genomes. *Nature, 531*, 156–159.

National Institutes of Health. (2003, April 14). *International Consortium Completes Human Genome Project.* https://www.genome.gov/11006929/.

Sanders, R. (2017, February 2). Doudna awarded Japan Prize for invention of CRISPR gene editing. *Berkeley News.* http://news.berkeley.edu.

Smith, C. (2017). Editing the editor: Genome editing gets a makeover with CRISPR 2.0. *Science, 355*(6321), 207–209. doi:10.1126/science.355.6321.210-c.

Travis, J. (2015). Making the cut: CRISPR genome-editing technology shows its power. *Science, 350*(6267), 1456–1457. doi:10.1126/science.350.6267.1456.

U. S. Department of Energy Office of Science. (2008). *Genomics and its impact on science and society: The human genome project and beyond* (DOE Publication No. SC-0083). http://web.ornl.gov/sci/techresources/Human_Genome/publicat/primer2001/primer11.pdf.

Yu, A. (2017, May 27). How a gene editing tool went from labs to a middle-school classroom. *National Public Radio.* http://www.npr.org.

Zimmer, C. (2016, June 3). Scientists find form of CRISPR gene editing with new capabilities. *The New York Times.* http://www.nytimes.com.

Chapter 7

Genome Development: Agricultural

Melodie Hunnicutt, Renie Johnston,
and John "Scott" Stauble Jr.

"The best way to predict the future is to invent it."

—Alan Kay

Genetic technology and genomics are not only affecting human life through medicine. In the field of agriculture, genetic technology is allowing for the alteration of crops and livestock at the level of their DNA to provide safer, more nutritious, and plentiful food supplies with hardier plant and animal species.

AGRIGENOMICS

Agriculture is the "science of breeding in crops and animals," a field vital to human survival in terms of global food production" (Illumina, Inc., 2016, p. 4). Due to the advances in genomic sequencing and typing during the last thirty years, including CRISPR-Cas9, this field has evolved into a agrigenomics, "the science of accelerating breeding decisions using whole genomic information" (Illumina Inc., 2016, p. 4).

This new field is revolutionizing how breeding decisions are made. It is also helping to monitor and protect wild plant and animal populations. Agrigenomic methodologies and tools are becoming ever more powerful and faster technologies that involve increased automation and produce more reliable results (Neuman, n.d.).

Continuing progress in agrigenomics is becoming more critical with every year as global climate change, decreasing availability of arable land, and worldwide population increases the demand for higher global levels of food production. Crops, as well as dairy and meat livestock, need to produce higher, more nutritious yields using less water and land, as well as fewer antibiotics and pesticides. In short, sustainable agricultural practices must be developed that take a far less toll on the environment (Neuman, n.d.).

One of the leaders in the agrigenomic revolution, Illumina, Inc., based in San Diego, California, began awarding an annual Greater Good Initiative Grant in 2011 to spur innovation and technological development in the field. These grant funds were intended "to help identify measures that can increase crop yields and improve livestock welfare and productivity to alleviate poverty and hunger in the developing world" (Neuman, n.d.).

The most recent recipient is the Donald Danforth Plant Science Center located in St. Louis, Missouri. Investigators there will partner with scientists at the Hudson Alpha Institute for Biotechnology in Huntsville, Alabama, to optimize breeding strategies for improving the yields and environmental tolerance of grain sorghum in Sub-Saharan Africa (Neuman, n.d.).

In addition to the breeding of plants and animals, agrigenomics is also used to analyze host pathogen interactions, increase genetic variation to preserve biodiversity, manage individually a specific animal or plant species of a particular value, and understand how genetic variability in a species reflects evolutionary adaptive changes due to environmental pressures. It can also be used to study the viruses that affect animal populations and the bacteria that live on and in them.

This can result in greater prevention and better treatment of disease outbreaks. For example, sequencing the intestinal bacteria of livestock animals can lead to research and improving animal feed in diagnosing infections. All of these genomic uses, however, also lead indirectly to the design of better breeding and selection programs (Illumina, Inc., 2016; Neuman, n.d.).

Greater food availability and quality are made possible through enhanced Genomic Selection (GS) in crop and animal breeding programs using genetic markers specific to individual species breeding populations. First described in 2001 by T. H. Meuwissen and his colleagues, GS operates on the principle that information from a large number of markers can be used to estimate breeding values. This eliminates that need for prior knowledge of where specific genes are located (Meuwissen, Hayes, and Goddard, 2001).

Advances in genetics, bioinformatics, and biotechnology have proven to be powerful tools for researchers and breeders in the development of GS techniques. They allow sequencing of a new species, meta-analysis of large data sets, and thus enhance the understanding of complex traits in animal and plant populations (Illumina, Inc., 2016).

The evolution of plant and animal populations in complex environments requires adaptation to adverse climate and soil conditions and predators. Being able to identify and learn about the genes underlying these adaptive traits in animal and plant species is invaluable in agrigenomics. The goal is to increase the most favorable traits in these populations to optimize food productivity and value (Illumina, Inc., 2016).

FROM MARKER ASSISTED SECTION (MAS) TO GENOMIC SELECTION (GS)

Marker Assisted Selection (MAS) of genetic traits is an old technique that dates back to the 1920s. MAS originally used morphological and biochemical markers in cells to indirectly select the genetic determinant(s) of a particular trait. It allowed identification of positive and negative selectable traits in animal and plant populations.

An example of a positive selectable marker would be disease resistance, while a negative selectable marker would be a trait that eliminates or inhibits the growth. Beginning in the 1980s with exponential advances in genomics, MAS began to use DNA-based markers (Brumlop and Finckh, 2010). MAS has been used to improve Holstein and Irish cattle breeding programs, to improve drought tolerance in hybrid strains of corn, and to improve disease and pest resistance in wheat, barley, rice, potato, tomato, soybean, and apple breeding (Illumina, Inc., 2016; Brumlop and Finckh, 2010).

Among the disadvantages of MAS are that most traits of agricultural value, especially in plant populations, are complex and single markers can explain only a small amount of the genetic variance. Thus, prediction of genetic effects overall tended to be low. The advent of GS has helped to overcome this limitation and resulted in much higher and accurate prediction models. GS is being used to improve grain crop yields and nutritional values in sub-Saharan Africa as described above (Illumina, Inc., 2016).

Advances in genomic sequence allowed the implementation of GS. This advanced technique allows breeders to select and breed the most promising animal and plant strains. Hundreds of genomes have now been sequenced and are publicly available in large databases. There has been substantial investment in DNA sequencing technologies over the last three decades.

Next-Generation Sequencing (NGS)

In 1990, the advent of Next-Generation Sequencing (NGS) has decreased the cost per genome by 100 million fold and led to economic advantages in animal breeding and plant selection. This has been particularly evident in cattle breeding programs in the agricultural biotechnology industry (Illumina, Inc., 2016).

Once an entire genome has been sequenced and assembled, it affords access to unique genomic markers in specific populations using DNA arrays. Advances in genotyping technologies now allow hundreds of thousands of genomic markers to be typed at the same time to create reference sequences.

These reference sequences can then be compared to other genomes to assess alignment. This has been utilized to grow improved strains of cotton, essential for both textile fiber and oilseed by-products. It is also especially useful in sequencing plant genomes, as they tend to be polyploid, having more than two paired sets of chromosomes, and thus more complex than diploid animal genomes (Illumina, Inc., 2016).

Although GS originally used a DNA array methodology, the development of genotyping by sequencing (GBS) has significant advantages over the array based method. GBS can create sequencing data in populations where spacing of markers is not available, and no reference genome exists. It also produces this data at reasonable prices. For example, GBS has been used to restore and better manage historical Columbia River basin salmon populations in Idaho (Illumina, Inc., 2016).

Specific GS Methodologies

This section lists and describes some of the most used GS techniques at the current time. The continuing evolution of the field in agrigenomics is powered by the rapid pace at which biotechnologies and bioinformatics are being developed and improved.

***De novo* plant and animal sequencing.** *De novo* plant and animal sequencing using Next Generation Sequencing (NGS) techniques is often the first step in investigating novel species or species that have not yet been sequenced ("Improving Breeding and Selection," n.d., para. 1). Called the "holy grail" ("*De Novo*," n.d., para. 1) of the sequencing technology, it has enabled researchers to reconstruct whole genomes at a fraction of the cost.

Its key attributes are the ability to resolve repeats in a DNS sequence and to distinguish between alleles and polyploid plant species. In some areas of animal and plant genomes, repetitive regions are no longer than active ones. NGS offers a cost-effective approach to link active regions and increase the continuity of the resulting genome (De Novo, n.d., para. 4–5).

Whole genome resequencing. This methodology is used when a plant or animal genome has already been sequenced, and a reference genome is thus available. It allows inspection and analysis of a genome at a micro level, enabling the discovery of specific genes in structural variants, as well as genotype determinations. This aids researchers in filling in gaps in the genomes of many plant and animal species, improves plant breeding and selection, and permits conclusive genomic comparisons between and within species ("Improving Breeding and Selection," n.d., para. 2).

It truly enables the completion of "all genetic tests in one" ("Whole Genome Resequencing," n.d., para. 1), revealing both large and small-scale variations in a plant or animal genome that might be missed otherwise because it gives a base by base view (Whole Genome Resequencing," n.d.).

Plant and animal epigenetics. As stated earlier, it is foundational to the field of agrigenomics to understand how plant and animal adaptations to environmental conditions, such as food access and drought conditions, drive changes in their phenotypes that affect the viability and reproductive success. Research in epigenetics help scientists deepen their understanding of how those factors control adaptation in a species of interest ("Improving Breeding and Selection," n.d., para. 3).

Since epigenetic changes to varying environmental situations affect adaptation on a large scale, they are a driving force in the growth and development of plant and animal species as well as their susceptibility to diseases (Understanding Epigenetic Modifications and Their Impact on Gene Regulation," n.d., para. 1).

Genotyping by sequencing. Genotyping by sequencing is also known as Next Generation Genotyping (NGG). This is a low-cost screening tool that allows scientists to discover new plant and animal Single Nucleotide Variations (SNVs) and genomes, as well as perform genotyping studies and genetic mapping. Because of the low financial investment, it offers a higher return on investment (ROI) for breeders.

Breeders can get purity testing on breeding strains and plant genome comparisons and evaluations. This is a significantly more economical way to study genetic variation and does not require a reference genome ("Improving Breeding and Selection," n.d., para. 6; "Sequence Based Genotyping Methods," n.d., para. 1–2).

Plant and animal transcriptome analysis. Transcriptome analysis is the sequencing of the complete Ribonucleic Acid (RNA) transcripts that are produced in any plant or animal genome. RNA is the nucleic acid molecule in cells that plays a vital role in the coding, decoding, regulation, and expression of genes. By sequencing the RNA in plant and animal genomes, researchers get valuable information regarding how gene expression levels change during the development of the organism, as well as how it responds to disease and stress ("Improving Breeding and Selection," n.d., para. 3).

Soil and agricultural metagenomics. This area of research is also known as environmental metagenomics, and it makes possible the study of large microbial communities in their natural environment without culturing. These studies produce critical information about diverse microbial populations that affect plant and animal development, such as those that enhance animal digestion or affect nitrogen content in the soil.

NGS is the methodology used in metagenomics; it allows for observation and tracking of a microbial adaptation over short periods of time in both the natural environment and laboratory ("Improving Breeding and Selection," n.d., para. 7). Using NGS, researchers can discover new organisms, as well as explore the dynamic life cycle of microbial populations.

Since microbes modify human, animal, and plant health, as well as support plant growth, it is vital to understand the roles they play in terrestrial and aquatic ecosystems. Scientists can then use this information to produce food, fuels, and chemicals that are more effective, efficient, and less harmful to the environment ("Metagenomics," n.d., para. 1).

COMMUNITY COLLEGE IMPACTS

The significance of agrigenomics will be enormous in community colleges throughout the nation that offer agricultural degrees and certificates. For example, Central Carolina Community College, in North Carolina, offers a Sustainable Agricultural Degree, Agricultural Sustainability Certificate, Sustainable Livestock Systems Certificate, and a Sustainable Vegetable Production Certificate ("Sustainable Agriculture," n.d., para. 1).

Other typical program areas that could be expected to be offered nationwide in community colleges located in major agribusiness states include: animal science, soil and crop sciences, agricultural production management, livestock management and merchandising and farm management. All of these degrees and certificate programs, regardless of where they are offered in the country, will need to be updated on an ongoing basis as the agrigenomic revolution progresses.

In South Carolina, agribusiness is the state's number one industry, generating 200,000 jobs from the 25,000 farms located throughout the state ("About," n.d., para. 17). The South Carolina Technical College System will need to encourage the creation of more of these programs especially in colleges located in high-volume agricultural geographic areas. Although this has not been a primary focus of technical colleges in the state, traditional farming and breeding methodologies and decision-making processes are being transformed by the introduction of more and more genomic information.

Advances in genetics, bioinformatics, and biotechnology as applied to agriculture will continue to become more sophisticated, and knowledge regarding their use will be critical to keep pace with other market competitors. It will be essential that South Carolina farmers be able to comprehend the genetic selection techniques and tests and use them to inform their farm management practices.

Short Term

In the present era of globally shared information, advances in technology have increased at an exponential pace. The democratization of information for the greater good has spurred a revolutionary period of discovery and application in the area of genomic research. In the last ten years, the number of articles pertaining to one part of genomic research, CRISPR, has accelerated in an especially sharp trajectory.

The potential for this technology now and in the future has wide ranging implications for all areas of society. In terms of personal medicine, genomic research will transform the way that medicine is practiced and treatments are developed. The growing human population of this planet has brought its own problems that must be solved to eliminate suffering while still maintaining ecological sustainability. This will require more efficient and effective use of arable land and aqua systems to produce sufficient levels of nutritious food through agrigenomics.

Mid Term

It is the community colleges expertise in workforce development and training that will be needed to support the innovation and spread of these genomic technological advances. The myriad of applications in medicine and agrigenomics will require a continually retrained labor force. Community colleges will be tasked with the ongoing monitoring and change in their program offerings and curriculum content to keep up with the pace of this explosive area of technology in terms of keeping students apprised of what they are going to be expected to know and be able to employ.

As the CRISPR results begin to impact diagnosis and treatments and more significant ways, healthcare programs will need to be continued constantly evaluated and tweaked to make sure that cutting edge information and training are being provided. The same will also hold for agricultural programs. Community colleges not only train in the skills needed for these career fields; they also spark interest in students.

Not all community college students are training for a career. College transfer students will be influenced by their studies at the community college level also. Community colleges can advance the future exploration of genomic technology by sparking the interest of future scientists.

Long Term

The advances in all forms of genomic research are tools that science can and will use to advance the human condition. The era of these breakthroughs and their applications has just begun. Community colleges are at the center of this web of discovery, and it will grow in its breath and complexity as more information is revealed when new questions are generated and answered. Status quo is not an option.

CONCLUSION

Humans have always been curious about themselves and their surroundings. This curiosity has led to the vast cultural, social, and scientific advances evident throughout their history. In an effort to discover more about themselves, humans have been only limited by the technology that is available and the boundaries of the human imagination.

REFERENCES

About. (n.d.). https://agriculture.sc.gov/about/.

Brumlop, S., & Finckh, M. R. (2010, December). *Applications and potentials of marker assisted selection (MAS) in plant breeding: Final report of the F+E project (FKZ 350 889 0020)*. Bonn, Germany: Federal Agency for Nature Conservation.

De Novo. (n.d.). http://igatechnology.com/genomics-research-services/plantanimal/de-novo-assembly/.

Illumina Announces Agricultural Greater Good Initiative Grant (2016, June 14). *TechnologyNetworks*. https://www.technologynetworks.com/tn/news/illumina-announces-agricultural-greater-good-initiative-grant-197700.

Illumina, Inc. (2016). *Genomic selection in agriculture*. https://www.illumina.com/content/dam/illumina-marketing/documents/products/research_reviews/genomic-selection-in-agriculture.pdf.

Improving Breeding and Selection. (n.d.). https://www.illumina.com/areas-of-interest/agrigenomics/plant-animal-sequencing.html.

Metagenomics. (n.d.). http://igatechnology.com/genomics-research-services/plantanimal/metagenomics/.

Meuwissen, T. H. E., Hayes, B. J., & Goddard, M. E. (2001). Prediction of total genetic value using genome-wide dense marker maps. *Genetics, 157*, 1819–1829.

Neumann, E. (n.d.). Agrigenomics: Tools for plant and animal breeding, fish and fowl [Web log comment]. http://www.tecan.com/blog/agrigenomics-probing-plant-and-animal-genomes.

Sequence-Based Genotyping Methods. (n.d.). https://www.illumina.com/techniques/sequencing/dna-sequencing/targeted-resequencing/genotyping-by-sequencing.html.

Sustainable Agriculture. (n.d.). http://www.cccc.edu/agriculture/.

Understanding Epigenetic Modifications and Their Impact on Gene Regulation. (n.d.). https://www.illumina.com/techniques/popular-applications/epigenetics.html.

Whole Genome Resequencing. (n.d.). http://igatechnology.com/genomics-research-services/whole-genomics-resequencing/.

Chapter 8

Nanotechnology

Anthony Dozier, Lonnie F. Griffin III, and Jaime McLeod

"It is change, continuing change, that is the dominant factor in society."

—Isaac Isimov

Across the landscape of the twenty-first century United States, wonderful and highly advanced technological innovations stand poised to radically change the lives of all Americans for generations to come. Nanotechnology is one area of applied science that has the promise to substantially change the world.

"Nanotechnologists foresee a second industrial revolution sweeping the world during our lifetimes as individual atoms are assembled together into thousands of useful new products" (Montague, 2004, p. 16). Higher education is spearheading this revolution, and the research labs with highly trained practitioners are drawn from the world of academia (Malsch, 2013).

This chapter provides an overview of nanotechnology, the current situation, future (short-, mid-, and long-term) changes in nanotechnology, future effects on community colleges, recommendations on programs that community colleges may need to add in the future, and general advice for community college leaders, faculty, staff, and students concerning the topic.

NANOTECHNOLOGY OVERVIEW

Understanding nanotechnology is akin to entering an entirely new world of scientific wonder where traditional rules of physics do not apply. As the Center for Responsible Nanotechnology (CRN, 2008) states, "Nanotechnology is the engineering of functional systems at the molecular scale" (p. 1). The nano world is governed by quantum physics and scientists must learn through experimentation the new properties and hazardous traits of materials as they

85

exist below 50 nanometers (Montague, 2004). At the nano level, materials behave in very unpredictable ways, and nano particles are small enough to pass through cell membranes (Robison, 2011).

The origin of nanotechnology goes back to the early 1800s when John Dalton pioneered the atomic theory of matter (Thurs, 2007). Richard Zsigmondy, the 1925 winner of the Nobel Prize in chemistry, developed the concept of a nanometer (Hulla et al., 2015). In 1959, Richard Feynman, the 1965 Nobel Prize winner in physics, gave a speech envisioning the theoretical capability of manipulating matter at the atomic level (Center for Responsible Nanotechnology, 2008).

"Nanotech is named for the nanometer, a unit of measure, 1 billionth of a meter, one thousandth of a micro meter" (Montague, 2004, p. 16). "Nanotechnology is defined as the understanding and control of matter at dimensions between one and 100 nm where the unique phenomena enable novel applications. . . ." (Hulla, Sahu, and Hayes, 2015, p. 1318).

Japanese engineer Norio Taniguchi independently coined the term nanotechnology in 1974 (Thurs, 2007). Montague (2004) notes that nano tech only became possible in the 1980s and early 1990s when individual atoms were able to be individually arranged by software controlled computers. The 1980s marked the beginning of the golden era of nanotechnology, and Eric Drexler of the Massachusetts Institute of Technology, using Taniguchi's term nanotechnology and ideas from Feynman, wrote a seminal book on the topic of nanotechnology in 1986 (Hulla et al., 2015).

Drexler's vision of nanotechnology, consisting of the idea of using nanoscale assemblers or nanobots to create anything desired from atoms, was extremely popular and pushed awareness of nanotechnology into the mainstream (Thurs, 2007). "The science of nanotechnology was advanced further when Iijima, another Japanese scientist, developed carbon nanotubes" (Hulla et al., 2015, p. 1318).

Nanotechnology and nanoscience stand poised to deliver on their promise of atomic engineering; however, with the rising concerns about the safety of nanotechnology, the difficulty of working in the nanoscale, and the debate about what nanotechnology means today, nanoscience is still in the early phases of development (Malsch, 2013).

CURRENT SITUATION

As Hulla et al., (2015) explain, "the beginning of the 21st century saw an increased interest in the emerging fields of nanoscience and nanotechnology" (p. 1318). In 2003, President George W. Bush signed the twenty-first-century Nanotechnology Research and Development Act, which granted $3.7 billion for research into nanoscale engineering and science over a period of four years (Thurs, 2007).

That legislation created the Nanotechnology Initiative (NNI) to prioritize nanotechnology research, and the NNI is managed at the cabinet level of the president (Hulla et al., 2015). "National security is one of the main priorities in the US National Nanotechnology Initiative and military nanotechnology receives structurally 30 percent of the federal NNI budget" (Malsch, 2013, p. 163). Montague (2004) notes that global private sector spending on nanotechnology is estimated at $3 billion and that governments are simultaneously spending the same amount.

Nanotechnology has been described as having four generations. The first generation, or current area, involves passive nanostructures, which includes materials designed to perform one task and products incorporating nanostructures (CRN, 2008). CRN (2008) reports the second generation, which is now emerging, introduces active nanostructures that allow sensors and drug delivery devices to be developed.

The third generation features nanosystems where thousands of components will interact at the nano level (CRN, 2008). The fourth generation, molecular nanosystems, will feature the first integrated nano system with hierarchical systems within systems operating much like a mammalian cell (CRN, 2008). The time line for culmination of all four generations is conservatively estimated at twenty to thirty years or more in the future (CRN, 2008).

The science of nanotechnology covers a large range of a mostly disconnected field. "According to the US National Science Foundation, national technology is the foundation stone of NBIC—a revolutionary convergence of nanotech, biotech (manipulation of genes), info tech (computers), and cogno tech (brain function)" (Montague, 2004, p. 17).

Obviously, nanotechnology has a great deal of potential application within NBIC and many other areas of science. Because of this potential to impact almost all industries, nanotechnology can be referred to as a general-purpose technology (CRN, 2008).

This means that nanotechnology is also a dual use technology with the ability to be used for commercial and military purposes (CRN, 2008). The end goal of nanotechnology would be the development of a personal nano factory that each household may one day possess to create the wide range of products people need in an efficient, rapid, and inexpensive manner (CRN, 2008).

While nanotechnology holds the promise of a brighter future, concerns over the use of this technology have been raised. Montague (2004) notes three criticisms with nanotechnology: the potential exists for a nano divide between those with access to this technology and those without; nano tech enhanced humans may gain an advantage over people who are not augmented, and corporations and individuals may gain monopoly control over nanotech items by patenting aspects of this technology.

Robison (2011) also notes three criticisms with nanotechnology: safety testing and regulation of nanotechnology devices are inadequate; nano-technology particles and artifacts are unpredictable, and nanoparticles and artifacts are capable of penetrating our bodies and lodging within our cells.

Concerns about safety led to the development of a nanotoxicology, the study of possible health consequences from nanoparticles, and nanomedicine, which researched the risks and benefits of nanomaterials used in medical devices and medical practice (Hulla et al., 2015). "In the environment, nano particles represent an entirely new class of pollutants with which scientists and nature have no experience" (Montague, 2004, p. 18).

THE FUTURE OF NANOTECHNOLOGY

What is the future of nanotechnology? What advances will be made in the scientific community in the short term, three to five years, the midterm, five to ten years, and the long term, ten to twenty years? Which ideas currently in research and development will be far enough along the spectrum to be suc-cessfully brought to market? Where will the government and private investors be willing to put their funding support? What potential safety hazards and ethical questions will be raised by this technological development?

These are some of the questions being asked and studied by the national Nanotechnology Initiative, a partnership of twenty federal agencies and cabi-net level departments with a common interest in nanotechnology research, development, and commercialization. Established in 2001, these agencies came together with a shared recognition that the ability to comprehend and harness nanoscale phenomena will be key to improving human health and quality of life, in addition to having a powerful impact on the American economy, job creation, and national defense.

Since NNI's inception, its member agencies have contributed over $23 billion of funding, used to support state-of-the-art research and world-class technological facilities for functions such as characterization, modeling, and fabrication. NNI resources have been a critical component to ensuring the responsible promotion of nanotechnology products from the laboratory to retail markets (NNI Strategic Plan, 2016).

The efforts and resources of NNI have led to many of the current applica-tions of nanotechnology and commercial products in the fields of electronics, cosmetics, healthcare, clothing, and automobiles. The United States Congress passed the twenty-first-century nanotechnology research and development act of 2003, requiring NNI agencies to develop a revised strategic plan every three years.

In October 2016, NNI submitted their most recent strategic plan to President Obama and Congress. The plan represents NNI member consensus on future priorities and gives a critical insight to the future direction of nanotechnology funding, consumer applications, and safeguards in the United States (NNI Strategic Plan, 2016).

Short Term

As opposed to singular, stand-alone technological achievements such as the Internet, nanotechnology advances are best described as complementary technological applications. For example, friction is the enemy of all mechanical parts. Friction hampers motion, causing eventual malfunctions in machines such as car engines, trains, and motors, as well as inefficiencies in facilities such as oil refineries and power plants (NNI Strategic Plan, 2016).

Imagine the ability to create machines with a near absence of friction, such as cars that require oil changes every three years, rather than every three months. Automobile engines would avoid breaking down for years, saving the public millions per year in maintenance and repair costs.

Funded by the Department of Energy as one of their five Nanoscale Science Research Centers (NSCRs), the Argonne researchers have proven that friction can be reduced on a macro scale in a dry environment by adding nano diamonds and graphene flakes between the surfaces of diamond like carbon and graphene coated silica. The graphene flakes form nanoscroll features, wrapping around the nano diamonds.

More and more flakes scroll over time, which incrementally reduces the contact area between the nano scrolls and the diamond-like carbon surface. This process eventually reduces the contact area between the surfaces by over 65 percent, dramatically reducing machine wear and tear. (NNI Strategic Plan, 2016). The implications of this superlubricity will have a great impact on reducing the cost of mechanical energy, as less power will be needed to operate machines.

Major nanotechnology innovations are also being developed in the medical field, and are very close to being ready for commercialization. Dr. Anthony Atala, the director of the Wake Forest Institute for Regenerative Medicine (WFIRM) at Wake Forest University, and Dr. Dwaine Davis, the department chair of physical sciences at Forsyth Community College, have formed a partnership with WFIRM to train employees on nanotech and biotech fundamentals to enhance their value to WFIRM, which would assist the wounded military veterans with lost limbs.

The Wounded Warrior Program Team is using nanotechnology to build scaffolding for a severed leg. There may be multiple techniques used to print cells. This would include nanotechnology and biotechnology. Within a few years this technology may provide tremendous opportunities to improve the lives of servicemen and women (Dr. Davis, personal communication, June 12, 2017).

Mid Term

Many nanotechnology applications are currently in research and development, requiring additional time in funding to resolve scientific problems standing between concept and marketplace. Among the various nanotechnology applications currently in the research phase, few will have more day-to-day impact on American public lives than cellulosic nanomaterials. In the next five to ten years cellulosic nano materials will transform the piece of fruit the college professor eats while driving to work, strengthen the concrete bridges on her route, and improve the insulation in her classroom (NNI Strategic Plan, 2016).

Cellulosic nanomaterials are derived from trees, giving them several advantages including being renewable and abundantly available with extraordinary properties. For example, cellulosic nanocrystals are lightweight but very strong, in addition to possessing electrical and optical properties.

The USDA Forest Service is driving the responsible commercialization of cellulosic nanomaterials for potentially hundreds of consumer applications. The Forest Service has a strategic approach, focusing the research and development capabilities of the USDA on solving the technical and economic barriers between these developing applications and the marketplace (NNI Strategic Plan, 2016).

Cellulosic nano materials may be used as a barrier coating for fruit, keeping the fruit intact and unspoiled for weeks at a time, even at room temperature (NNI Strategic Plan, 2016). The implications of this breakthrough are immense.

It could reduce tons of wasted produce in grocery stores, extend the life of fruit within the customer's home, improve the ability to ship fresh produce to impoverished areas across the country, and improve the capabilities of international and domestic trade where fruit crops were previously too perishable to ship. The cost savings to restaurants and related food services from improved storage and reduced waste would be significant (NNI Strategic Plan, 2016).

In addition, cellulosic nanomaterials are being applied to concrete, resulting in a stronger, more durable product. High-strength aerogels are being formed from cellulosic nanomaterials, which will provide improved insulation for housing and commercial real estate. Another application and development is the use of nanomaterials in reinforced paper products, the nanomaterials providing improved strength and durability (NNI Strategic Plan, 2016).

Long Term

In the next ten to twenty years, nanotechnology will have tremendous impacts in the field of medicine, specifically in creating new approaches to combating humanity's greatest health threats (NNI Strategic Plan. 2016). Imagine nanotechnology capable of entering the human bloodstream and seeking out and destroying cancer cells throughout the body in a matter of days.

Or, imagine nanotechnology sentinels residing in the human body, proactively patrolling for new cancer cells in patients with the genetic markers or a cancer history, springing into action when cells are detected. What impact would nanotechnology that can detect and eliminate traces of HIV in the body have on society? At a minimum, deadly diseases would shift toward becoming chronic, manageable conditions, or in the best-case scenario, these diseases would become as treatable as high blood pressure.

In October 2015, the Nanotechnology Startup Challenge (NSC) in cancer research was launched, a group collaboration between the National Cancer Institute (NCI), the Center for Advancing Innovation (CAI), and Medimmune. The purpose of the NSC is to speed up the commercialization of nanotechnology innovations specifically intended for cancer applications. The NSC accomplishes this by recruiting young entrepreneurs and college students to launch startup companies capable of commercializing these disk discoveries (NNI Strategic Plan, 2016).

Initially eight promising nanotechnology inventions from various scientists in the National Institute of Health (NIH) were selected; however, teams were invited to bring in additional external technologies for the competition. In April 2016, a total of twenty-eight teams made up of 274 scientists, entrepreneurs, business experts, and legal professionals, were accepted into the Nanotechnology Startup Challenge.

Competing teams were set up for success, as CAI required participation in accelerator training, providing teams with business development coaching from experts from various biotechnology industries, venture capitalists, government officials, and foundation representatives (NNI Strategic Plan, 2016).

One of the winning teams formed AuTACA, a startup company from the Wake Forest School of Medicine. The Nanotechnology Startup Challenge has created a pathway to commercializing cancer nanotechnology, building an innovative model for other organizations and investors to use to bring nanotechnology advances to market, and ultimately save lives (NNI Strategic Plan, 2016).

In the long-term future of nanotechnology there will need to be a great deal of focus on retraining programs for engineers and other technology professionals. Just as engineers over the last three decades were retrained in the latest generation of computer language, tomorrow's multidisciplinary engineers will require training on how to integrate the latest nanotechnology advances into their jobs. This need presents a unique opportunity for community colleges to build specific programs to deliver this training (Dr. Davis, personal communication, June 12, 2017).

THE ETHICS OF NANOTECHNOLOGY

As important as any new nanotechnology discovery on the horizon will be, the coordinated commitment to ethical and responsible handling of nanotechnology at every level of development and commercialization is critical. The NNI includes one of its four core goals as, "support responsible development of nano technology" (NNI Strategic Plan, 2016).

The collection of agencies recognizes the importance of protecting the environment and that human health must remain a priority, while nanotechnology development and commercialization continue to benefit society (NNI Strategic Plan, 2016).

When dealing with particles not visible to the naked eye, concerns of contamination to the human body are real, and precautionary practices and processes must be developed. Just as nanotechnology technicians must wear personal protective equipment to keep carbon nanotubes from entering their lungs, skin, and eyes, the public must be protected from the potential mishaps of in adequate nanotechnology disposal or corporate negligence, due to either lack of expertise or a desire to avoid costs.

Strong governmental regulations will be needed at the state and federal levels to ensure the safety of nanotechnology workers and the public. These legislations will need to be both multidisciplinary and international in their scope and coordination (NNI Strategic Plan, 2016).

EFFECTS ON COMMUNITY COLLEGES

Nanotechnology is a global industry with the potential to significantly impact everyone over the coming decades. The potential benefits and jobs created from nanotechnology innovations are almost limitless. Community colleges must track the progress of nanotechnology and its impact on the business community and jobs.

There are no forms of higher education more capable of training the emerging nanotechnology workforce than community colleges. A wave of potential students is on the horizon, but it will require a degree of preparation by institutional leadership. The arrival date of specific and nano particle innovations cannot be predicted with certainty. However, when the changes occur the demand will be intense.

Short Term

Dong, Gao, Sinko, Zaisheng, Jiango, and Lee (2016) note the hype behind nanotechnology is significant and state that many scientists feel a breakthrough is close. Areas that are on the brink of important discoveries include "nanomaterial based diagnostics imaging, complementation of diagnostic tools combined with therapeutic modalities, and nano carriers of biotechnology" (Dong et al., 2016, p. 8). According to Dong et al., the United States is the leader in publishing nanotechnology research, but China is not far behind.

The national nanotechnology initiative has funded over $170 billion worth of nanotechnology research (Dong et al., 2016). The need to fine tune nanotechnologies is great, as nanotechnology holds the rare potential of altering nearly every industry on the planet. Every study produces the opportunity to create a new industry or an improvement to an existing product. The key to understanding how to thrive in a world utilizing nanotechnology is education, partnerships, patience, and action. Community colleges that follow these practices have a bright future.

Nanotechnology is already having an impact on community colleges in the United States, even though the technology is still in the early stages of development. The nano.gov website lists twenty-six programs in nanotechnology in community colleges across the United States and Puerto Rico. Programs at these community colleges include certificates, technical associate degrees, and transfer opportunities to four-year universities.

Mid Term

Graduating students are employed in government, manufacturing, and scientific services. In 2012, 68,000 people were working in the field of nanotechnology. The field is expected to grow by over 20 percent by 2022. The expanding employment opportunities offer a growth area for community colleges to respond to and prepare for. The majority of jobs and training in nanotechnology are technician positions, ideally suited for community college programs.

A tour of the Center for Nanotechnology and Molecular Materials at Wake Forest University provides an excellent overview of the current state of nanotechnology mostly found in small research offices. Nanotechnology at the Center is currently in a state of research and development, with staff actively testing new ideas.

Researchers have numerous theories and concepts they wish to test, but few of these ideas have a guaranteed short-term return on investment, making it difficult to retain private investors. Research in nanotechnology is still in its early phase, which makes predicting the end state of the technology difficult.

Community colleges should keep a close eye on the developments in the field of nanotechnology, such as the need for qualified technicians to operate and perform maintenance on the necessary machines and instruments such as electron microscopes, or the need to write and operate software coding necessary to conduct atomic scale work. Community college leaders need to build close relationships with nanotechnology researchers, incorporating their input into the college's strategic planning while the technology innovations continue to develop.

Forsyth Technical Community College (FTCC) in Winston-Salem, North Carolina, partners with Wake Forest University and the University of North Carolina at Greensboro to provide nanotechnology education to their students as an example of how nanotechnology students are employed, Dr. Dwaine Davis of FTCC sees opportunities for nanotechnology students to obtain jobs in the paint industry (D. Davis, personal communication, June 12, 2017).

Nanotechnology can assist paint manufacturers in creating a durable paint that is more resistant to rust and chipping. Dr. Davis sees nanotechnology as a research topic that is linked to other technologies rather than an independent technology (D. Davis, personal communication, June 12, 2017).

The impact of nanotechnology on industry and community colleges is currently limited by a lack of knowledge by the public regarding the potential benefits of nanotechnology innovations. More investments are needed by the private sector to further the advances of the research, and there is a need to re-energize the funding pool (D. Davis, personal communication, June 12, 2017). Until the amount of research funding increases, nanotechnologies' intermediate term impact on community colleges is restricted.

Long Term

One of the effects on community colleges over the next ten to twenty years will be the retraining of the current engineering workforce in nanotechnologies (D. Davis, personal communication, June 12, 2017). Engineers currently working in the field have limited training and community colleges excel at short-term workforce training, which could meet that need. There is also an opportunity to train newly graduated engineers who did not receive nanotechnology skills in their undergraduate degree.

COMMUNITY COLLEGE PROGRAMS

Foothill College in Los Altos, California, provides an excellent example of the current offerings for nanotechnology at community colleges. Students have the choice of three separate career paths and study under instructors who conduct research for the National Aeronautics and Space Administration (NASA) ("Nanotechnology," n.d.).

The three paths Foothill College offers include a technician track, a traditional engineering track, and training for professional engineers to upgrade their skill set. If a community college desires to add nanotechnology to its offerings, these are the three most common types of programs that could be implemented currently.

A technician track is a common offering in nanotechnology at community colleges. These programs are generally two year degrees that are designed for students looking for entry-level technician positions. Technicians work under the supervision of an engineer and use equipment that produces nanomaterial. The degree program also prepare students to assist researchers with inspections and documentation.

The traditional engineering track offers students seeking an engineering degree the chance to take nanotechnology classes while attending community college. Students then transfer to university programs in engineering. Nanotechnology classes help attract students into engineering classes at community colleges who might otherwise take only traditional transfer courses. Exposing nanotechnology to transfer students will help community colleges provide better service to students seeking an engineering transfer degree.

One of the most exciting benefits of nanotechnology for community colleges is training professional engineers. Many practicing engineers have no educational background in nanomaterials. They were trained before nanotechnology techniques became more refined, if they were trained in the field at all. As the field of nanotechnology grows to reach most industries, current engineers will need training to utilize the innovations.

For example, a mechanical engineer building high-speed assembly machines will need to understand how to negotiate the new superlubricity features of the latest machine line he is working to improve and how they will impact the finished product. A great need for short-term training presents a perfect opportunity for community colleges to reach out to a new population of adult, professional students.

Short Term

In the short term, community colleges can begin training their current engineering faculty in nanotechnology. Once the engineering faculty have experience, community colleges need to partner with researchers and utilize their facilities for student instruction. Community colleges can offer their students internships to create a mutually beneficial partnership with a university or business. Forsyth Technical Community College uses this model to train students through a partnership with Wake forest University.

New programs and nanotechnology will not come without drawbacks. Biradar, Kadam, Chintale, Halle, and Maske (2013) describe Biomedical Nanotechnology as an area of study that is rapidly growing in popularity in research studies. Working with nano-sized particulars not only can lead to ethical dilemmas but it can also expose students to the potential hazards of nanotubes.

Certain nanotechnology procedures require the student to interact with nanotubes. A report from the CDC notes there are many uncertainties when determining the risks associated with carbon nanotubes and nano fibers (Department of Health and Human Services, 2013, p. vi). Community colleges must promote safety and monitor research on the danger of using these materials.

Mid Term

For nanotechnology utilization that extends beyond the short term, community colleges should build on the existing relationships they have with businesses and create direct pathways into the workforce. As time passes, more technical programs will use nanotechnology. Medical, agriculture, and manufacturing are just a few of the potential industries that will benefit from nanotechnology innovation.

The future for nanotechnologies integration into a broad spectrum of industries is bright. Community colleges should prepare for the intermediate and long-term future by starting small and building partnerships to ensure they are ready as nanotechnology rapidly expands in the future.

Long Term

The growth of nanotechnology in the last few decades is different than any industry innovations of the past. New technology often phases out industry that are aging; however, nanotechnology has the potential to revive industry programs instead of deleting them. Nanotechnology adds a new improvement to material science and introduces a new scale of size and potential.

Instead of causing other programs at community colleges to decrease, nanotechnology breathes new life into technical engineering education such as architecture, engineering, and civil services. Nanotechnology also requires students to have a knowledge of chemistry and biology.

Nanotechnology will require classes and programs to become more up to date and train students on the nanoscale as an additional requirement.

Community colleges need to incorporate nanotechnology content into existing science courses. The sooner it is integrated into the science courses, the easier it will be to create certificate and degree programs that meet the needs of nanotechnology students.

As nanotechnology creeps into all industries across the community college program spectrum, many technical programs will soon include nanotechnology courses. The immediate need for change to nanotechnology is not pressing, but the transition is more inevitable with every year that passes.

Entire new classes of jobs will be created, dependent upon which innovation proves to be the most successful in the open market. Community college leaders should view nanotechnology as a technology that enhances programs all across campus. Leaders should prepare for a nanotechnology invasion across many campus disciplines over the next ten to twenty years.

CONCLUSION

Exploring nanotechnology provides insight into the future of higher education and technology. "Most interest in and the willingness to commit financial and material resources to nanotechnology have often followed from a belief that it will change the world for the better in coming decades" (Thurs, 2007, p. 251). While research involving nanotechnology is still in its early phase, which makes predicting the technology difficult, community colleges should keep a close eye on the developments in this field.

Community college leaders must develop close partnerships with nanotechnology researchers while the technological innovations continue to develop and mature into viable commercial products, similar to the partnership between Forsyth Technical Community College and Wake Forest University. Existing technology instructors must be trained in nanotechnology, and new hires with prior background knowledge of this area should be given consideration.

The keys to understanding the future of nanotechnology are education, partnerships, research, and strategic patience. The knowledge gained concerning nanotechnology in higher education will position the next generation of community college leaders to be successful partners with business and industry for decades to come.

REFERENCES

Biradar, G. O., Kadam, A. G., Chintale, P. D., Halle, M. K., & Maske, K. S. (2013). A comprehensive review on nanotechnology. *Research Journal of Pharmacy and Technology*, 6(5), 486–495.

Center for Responsible Nanotechnology. (2008). *What is nanotechnology?* http://www.crnano.org/whatis.htm.

Department of Health and Human Services. (2013, April). Occupational Exposure to Carbon Nanotubes and Nanofibers (Publication No. 2013–145). The Centers for Disease Control and Prevention, https://www.cdc.gov/niosh/docs/2013-145/pdfs/2013-145.pdf.

Dong, H., Gao, Y., Sinko, P. J., Zaisheng, W., Jiango, X., & Lee, J. (2016). The nanotechnology race between China and the United States. *Nano Today, 11*, 7–12.

Hulla, J. E., Sahu, S. C., & Hayes, A. W. (2015). Nanotechnology: History and future. *Human and Experimental Toxicology, 34*(12), 1318–1321.

Malsch, I. (2013). Governing nanotechnology in a multi-stakeholder world. *Nanoethics, 7*, 161–172.

Montague, P. (2004). Welcome to nanoworld: Nanotechnology and the precautionary principle imperative. *Multinational Monitor, 25*(9), 16–19.

Nanotechnology. (n.d.). https://foothill.edu/sli/nanotechnology.html.

NNI Strategic Plan. (2016). National Nanotechnology Initiative Strategic Plan. https://www.nano.gov/sites/default/files/pub_resource/2016-nni-strategic-plan.pdf.

Robison, W. L. (2011). Nanotechnology, ethics, and risks. *Nanoethics, 5*, 1–13.

Thurs, D. P. (2007). Building the nano-world of tomorrow: Science fiction, the boundaries of nanotechnology, and managing depictions of the future. *Extrapolation, 48*(2), 244–267.

Chapter 9

Bitcoin and Blockchain

Darrel W. Staat

"Our lives are being converted to data."

—Garry Kasparov

There are new currency and banking concepts developing mostly in the background without a great deal of fanfare. Although Bitcoin, a digital currency, and Blockchain, a digital recording system, have been around for about a decade, they are not well known to most Americans. The two concepts together provide an alternative financial system that could, if mainstreamed, compete directly with the current banking system (Tapscott, D., & Tapscott, A., 2016).

At present they exist off to the side without presenting any real issues to the existing financial system of banks and currency. However, some major banking institutions are studying the system and piloting some projects to see how things work out. However, since both are technologies, they could be significantly influenced by Moore's Law, which predicts that computer power, doubles every eighteen months. So, as time passes, a new system of banking and currency could expand in an exponential fashion.

THE BITCOIN/BLOCKCHAIN MODEL

At present, the possibility of a new financial system developing may seem almost impossible; however, one must remember that if the Bitcoin/Blockchain model were to develop exponentially, it would take time before it could be seen as actual competition to the current banking system and currency processes. It would follow the hockey stick metaphor with apparently very little change for years and then suddenly, if one is not aware of its existence, jump onto the scene with tremendous velocity.

As a comparison, recall the cell phone developing from bag phone to smartphone in less than twenty years, followed by the fact that today's smartphones are computers in their own right, which become extremely more powerful each year, thanks to Moore's Law.

At the moment, currencies are usually directly connected to countries, although the Euro is a currency connected to a number of European countries rather than a single one. In the past, currency was made from metal and paper, which were exchanged for real products and services. The process worked reasonably well for centuries with the exception of something like counterfeit paper money.

However, with the advent of the digital age, money in the banking system has been digitalized, that is to say, money has become a series of numbers viewed on a printout. Although one can still go to the bank and obtain actual paper money, it is not a requirement. Today one can buy products or pay bills with a computer or cell phone without any paper or coin money changing hands.

The alternative of merely switching numbers for goods and services has caught on with the millennial generation who rarely carry cash. For that matter, they do not need to carry credit or debit cards either since their cell phone has the ability to place funds into their bank account and transfer funds to retail establishments to pay for goods and services. This digitalization is an initial step toward the possibility of not using cash for any transactions. Digitalization brings to the foreground that currency exists in terms of numbers only.

> Bitcoin is a "digital currency;" one that is stored in code and traded online. It is also a "cryptocurrency," a term that is often used interchangeably with digital currency but signifies that the currency uses cryptographic methods in an attempt to make it secure (Ross, 2016, p. 98).

Bitcoin was released during the great recession of 2008 as a result of declining trust in the existing financial system, which had been part and parcel of some of the issues leading to the recession (Ross, 2016). Already in 2014, Bitcoin could be used as currency in a number of businesses such as Victoria's Secret, Amazon, eBay, Kmart and more. The use will most likely expand considerably each year.

When one purchases Bitcoin, no paper or coin will be received; rather, the owner will receive a slot on a ledger with the amount purchased in Bitcoin. The transaction and ownership are kept in a secret, cryptographic secure ledger which can only be activated with a private key owned by the individual (Tapscott, D., & Tapscott, A., 2016).

The owner knows where his/her Bitcoins are located and can access them using the private key. The ledger, which holds the Bitcoins, is called a

Blockchain. It holds all the transactions that are logged using the private key of the owner. The Blockchain stores every transaction going back to the first one (Gates, 2017).

The Blockchain might best be understood as a cloud ledger that holds all transactions made. It is cryptographically secured. Further, the entire ledger is available to every Bitcoin user. Since it is public, it reduces the possibility of fraud (Ross, 2016).

Bitcoin/Blockchain is one example of an alternative financial system that already exists; others also exist or are in development. Since this alternative financial method is developing in an exponential manner, Bitcoin/Blockchain, or other alternative financial systems, may become the new financial systems used throughout the world in the future.

Short Term

How soon could this kind of alternative financial system become totally available? The closest predicted date is 2025. The World Economic Forum has research to indicate that date as a turning point (Schwab, 2016). It could happen that fast or it could take another decade depending on how consumers worldwide accept the new system(s) and how well the cryptographic security system actually work over time.

There are many critics of the Bitcoin/Blockchain system. Some think that security will be an issue that could bring the entire process down. Others call it a Ponzi scheme or a process to be used by the criminal element. Still others believe that gold will remain the foundation of the financial system and technology will not be able to overcome it (Gates, 2017).

Long Term

Some on Wall Street think the Blockchain system has real potential and are already using it in pilot stock transactions. Time will certainly tell whether the alternative financial system will work satisfactorily, but one must be aware that the beginnings of the system exist. As Moore's Law comes into play, the alternative financial system(s) will appear as if almost nothing is happening for a number of years and then, suddenly they could become a major player in the financial world.

IMPACT ON COMMUNITY COLLEGES

How would this new method of finance affect community colleges? In simplest terms, the student may want to pay tuition with a Bitcoin and the college will need to be ready to accept that payment. The state in which the college is located may choose to use an alternative financial system which would cause the institution to completely revise its local financial processes. Most likely that change will not happen soon, but there could be a relatively short transition period of moving from traditional currency to a new model in the future.

When it does, the business programs of the college would need to modify their courses to include the alternative financial method. The faculty and staff may be paid in Bitcoin and will have to receive training on how that method works. Another effect might be that the existing banking systems are forced to close up or determine new missions and directions. Whether that happens remains to be seen.

It is important that the community college leaders are aware of the potential changes that could affect the college, possibly in the near future. Being on the lookout will help leaders to understand what is coming and how quickly it will need to be incorporated into the financial processes and course offerings at the institution.

REFERENCES

Gates, M. (2017). *Blockchain: Ultimate Guide to Understanding Blockchain, Bitcoin, Cryptocurrencies, Smart Contracts, and the Future of Money.* Self-Published.

Ross, Alec. (2016). *The Industries of the Future.* New York: Simon & Schuster.

Schwab, Klaus. (2016). *The Fourth Industrial Revolution.* Geneva: World Economic Forum.

Tapscott, D., & Tapscott A. (2016). *Blockchain Revolution: How Technology Behind Bitcoin is Changing Money, Business, and the World.* New York, NY: Penguin Random House.

Chapter 10

Quantum Computing

Darrel W. Staat

"It's a bit like trying to balance an egg at the end of a needle."

—Jerry Chow

QUANTUM THEORY

During the early twentieth century, Max Planck and Albert Einstein led the research into the quantum world. A plethora of other scientists and mathematicians worked diligently to understand the quantum world, an existing world which is very different from the everyday world observed through the five senses. In the observable world, "everything appears to have a definite position, definite momentum, definite energy, and a definite time of occurrence" (Kisak, 2016).

The quantum world, which operates in the arena of atoms, is one that takes the mind of a physicist to fully understand. It was found that in the quantum world the theories of Isaac Newton were useless. His theories explain how things work in the everyday world, but they do not explain how things operate in the environment the quantum world, where an atom can exist in two locations at the same time.

Something existing in two locations at the same time does not make any sense in the observable world, but in the quantum world, the smallest world of atoms and molecules, it does make sense. By the way, even Albert Einstein had trouble getting his arms around the quantum world, but in the long run of the decades of the twentieth century, other scientists proved the theory to be true, repeatedly, and conclusively (Nicas, 2017, p. 4).

BITS AND QUBITS

Whereas the bits that the classical computer uses are 0 and 1, each of which exist individually, in the quantum computer, which uses atoms, a new term was developed to describe how it works: qubits. In the qubit the 0 and 1 exist simultaneously in two places at the same time. That dual location is called superposition. According to Jack Nicas (2017), "in the classical computer, bits are like coins that display heads or tails. Qubits on the other hand, are like coins spinning through the air in a coin toss showing both sides at the same time" (p. 4).

The qubit's ability to be in two locations simultaneously can be harnessed to process information exponentially faster than bits in a classical computer. "The computing power of a data center stretching blocks could theoretically be achieved by a quantum chip the size of a period at the end of this sentence" (Nicas, 2017, p. 4).

THE CLASSICAL COMPUTER AND THE QUANTUM COMPUTER

How do we best understand the difference in output between the classic computer we use daily and a quantum computer? Linus Chang, the founder of the software company SCRAM in Melbourne, Australia, provides this example. "If it takes a classical computer one day to crack a particular 56 bit encryption, it would take a quantum computer just 0.322 milliseconds, or 1000's of the blink of an eye" (Johnson, 2017, p. 14A).

Robert Miller claims that "researchers have estimated that a quantum computer has the potential to perform the equivalent of all human thought since the dawn of our species in a tiny fraction of a second" (Miller, 2011).

Just as we are getting used to Moore's Law in the twenty-first century, we are now faced with a new exponential velocity that is almost impossible to understand. The possible effects of quantum computing on the world as we know it are beyond belief, but real. Quantum computing is heading toward the world of computing like a tsunami. It is critical that scientists in the United States conduct research into this quantum possibility, if for no other reason than the fact that China is moving ahead full speed into the world of quantum computing.

QUANTUM COMPUTING INTERNATIONALLY

In Hefei, Anhui Province in China, a $10 billion, 4,000,000 SF facility is being constructed to house a research center for quantum applications (China Daily, 2017, October 19). This facility is slated to open in 2020 with two goals, quantum metrology and quantum computing (Lin and Singer, 2017). Such a facility could push China at phenomenal speed far ahead of other nations in the world of quantum computing.

The facility could support military projects, defense, and civilian innovators. Current reports predict that quantum computing could become a widespread reality by 2025 (Johnson, 2017). There is no doubt that quantum computing could in a matter of a decade change everything we know as normal in today's computing world and beyond.

QUANTUM COMPUTING AND THE SINGULARITY

For business and industry, quantum computing will present possibilities not even considered in our current, rapidly changing world. The singularity, the possibility of an Artificial Super Intelligence (ASI), could become reality even faster than the predictions of Ray Kurzweil, who has stated that the ASI is a real possibility by 2045 just by using Moore's Law, the doubling of current computing power every eighteen months. He suggests that we might have to deal with a computer mind with an IQ of 6000 (Kurzweil, 2005).

With a quantum computer, the singularity might more likely have an IQ of 1 million; however, that is anybody's guess. James Barratt (2013) in his book, *Our Final Invention: Artificial Intelligence and the End of the Human Era*, sees only phenomenal danger with the increased ability of the ASI computer. Oddly enough, he does not even consider quantum computing in his book; his concern comes from classical computing power doubling every eighteen months, a far cry from quantum computing potential.

EFFECTS ON COMMUNITY COLLEGES

Will community colleges still exist in a world with quantum computing? That is a good question. It is hard to see around the corner without an exponential periscope. Will community colleges still be needed? Woodrow Barfield, author of *Cyber Humans: Our Future with Machines*, has a possible response.

He starts his book with "a controversial and bold statement, our future is to merge with artificially intelligent machines" (Barfield, 2015, p. 1). He argues that

> the merging of humans with machines could benefit humans in a number of ways: for example, by swapping our biology for non-biological parts we could gain the ability to automatically repair or replace to prosthesis, including narrow prosthesis when damaged or outdated (Barfield, 2015, p. 41).

Short and Mid Term

What about community colleges? In the near future will we teach students to learn in medical fields that we do not even know about today? Will we teach students how to build everything they will need in their lives with 3D printing? Will our faculty provide instruction in the field of personal robots, autonomous cars, genome agriculture and the Internet of Things?

Long Term

For example, nanotechnology could produce the need for creative, critical thinking individuals that community colleges would be teaching. Further, what about welders, plumbers, electricians, HVAC technicians, and others? Do they disappear replaced by robots?

What about leaders? It would seem that the world, nations, states, cities, towns, and communities will need people who can see the big picture, who care about others, and who have a positive vision for the future. Quantum computing could have impacts and effects on everything. Just how to deal with it will take creative, inventive minds.

CONCLUSION

As administrators, faculty, staff, students, business and community leaders, we all need to be aware of the future exponential possibilities. We will need to learn how to deal with them for the benefit of all concerned. We may play a more crucial role in the future than we do today with eyes open, minds prepared, ready to lead in a variety of areas. It will be a day-by-day journey, making changes as we proceed. We must be prepared to jump into new directions as the environment changes. We must be ready for anything and everything.

REFERENCES

Barfield, Woodrow. (2015). *Cyber-Humans: Our Future with Machines.* New York: Springer.

Barrat, James. (2013). *Our Final Invention: Artificial Intelligence and the End of the Human Era.* New York: St. Martin's Press.

China Daily. (2017, October 19). News. No title. Chinadaily.com.cn.

Johnson, T. (2017, October 22). News. Hyper computers are coming—and they'll see past your flimsy security. *The State,* 14A.

Kisak, P., ed. (2016). *An Overview of Quantum Computing: The State of the Art in Computers.* USA: Createspace.com.

Kurzweil, Ray. (2005). *The Singularity is Near.* New York: Penguin.

Lin, J., & Singer, P. W. (2017, October 10). The country wants to build a quantum computer with a million times the computing power of all others present in the world. *Popular Science.*

Miller, R. (2011, December 8). Hardware. Quantum computing: What is it and has it arrived? *Tech Decision Maker.*

Nicas, J. (2017). Ideas. How Google's quantum computer could change the world. *Wall Street Journal.* hppts://www.wsj.com/articles/how-googles-quantum-computer-could-change-the-world.

Chapter 11

Exponential Leadership

Darrel W. Staat

"Higher education, like all of us, will have to adapt."

—Joseph Aoun

THE EXPONENTIAL PROCESS

Since most technologies in the future will change in an exponential manner, whether using Moore's Law or quantum computing, rather than a linear method, it is critical that community college leaders in the twenty-first century become aware of what technologies are heading toward them and when they might appear.

As this book has shown, it will be important to understand that changes on the periphery that appear to be moving incrementally may, in fact, not be following a linear path. Rather, they may be developing at an exponential rate of change, like the penny doubling example, which did not show immediate increases while it was developing, but later seemed to appear out of nowhere.

The chapters in this book demonstrated that AI, autonomous vehicles, personal robots, 3D printing, the Internet of Things, nanotechnology, genome research, bitcoin/blockchain, and quantum computing all develop in a seemingly linear fashion for a period of time, but then jump up with exponential velocity.

How do those leading community colleges in a time of exponential change guide their institutions in a viable and successful direction for the benefit of faculty, staff, students, the business community and local economic development? That question will have to be answered often, quickly and accurately.

Successful community college leadership in the twenty-first century will demand a great deal of effort because community college leaders in the very near future will very soon have to start thinking as exponential leaders. They will need to understand the college in ways very different from the past while continuing the basic mission of the institutions.

EXPONENTIAL THINKING

Exponential thinking involves continuous updating on developments in technology, continually researching the needs of the local business community, rapidly resetting the college vision, accurately providing the development of the faculty/staff, quickly obtaining the latest equipment and, in general, rapidly learning to deal with the increased velocity of change.

At present, community college leaders may tend to think in linear terms; however, the technology of the twenty-first century does not operate that way. Instead, it develops exponentially like the hockey stick metaphor, linearly with some incremental increases for a portion of its beginning development until it reaches a point where it suddenly increases in an almost vertical direction.

Community college leaders, who want to work successfully in the coming decades when the world, the college, the business community, local economic development and, most importantly, the students, become caught up in a tsunami-like set of events, will need to completely change the way they think and understand the world they live in. What will it take?

Continual Research and Updating

To deal with exponential change, community college leaders will have to be continuously updated on what is happening in all technologies that are identified to have exponential potential. Leaders will need to understand where the technological developments stand on a monthly basis for some, quarterly for others and annually for a few.

For example, the leaders will need to be updated monthly in terms of 3D printing, the Internet of Things, autonomous vehicles, drones, bitcoin/blockchain, and personal robots. All of those technologies are ready to take the exponential leap forward. Quarterly updates will be needed on genome developments and Artificial Intelligence. Semi-annual updates will be needed on nanotechnology and quantum computing. In addition, the leaders will need to be on the lookout for new technologies that could spring up at any time.

The important thing is to have all of the possibilities on the research list followed through with regular, periodic updates. Leaders need to know, as best as can be predicted, when the technologies will hit the extreme uptick. One futurist believes that leaders should go back to school every year (Uldrich, 2007). Not likely to happen in a linear world, but what about an exponential one? Rather than going back to school, why not bring the school to you?

Community college leaders must position themselves at the forefront of the change if they are interested in keeping their colleges successful. Community colleges will need to be prepared to jump into the breech in terms of the training and education needed for the workforces involved. The mission of education for individuals, training for the business community and support of local economic development will demand it.

RESEARCHING THE LOCAL BUSINESS COMMUNITY

The Internet of Things

It is critical that the college president, members of the administration, and faculty research the workforce needs of the local business community in an organized and continuous manner to keep up with the latest technological developments. For example, the Internet of Things may invade many businesses that in turn will need to stay abreast of developments that might further affect their enterprises. Some businesses may see opportunities created by the IoT and move ahead expeditiously in those directions. The college will need to be prepared to support those efforts.

3D Printing, Personal Robots, Autonomous Vehicles, Bitcoin/ Blockchain, and Genome Developments

The same kind of change could happen with 3D printing, personal robots, autonomous vehicles, bitcoin/blockchain, and genome research. These technologies are all poised to expand exponentially and could have rapid, powerful impacts on the business community in the United States and abroad.

It is critical that community college leaders be receptive to the data that is gathered on directions taken by the business community, even if at times, it is counter intuitive (Uldrich, 2007). If the college is interested remaining viable and successful in its mission, continual research to determine the workforce needs of the business community will become extremely critical in the age of exponential development.

Nanotechnology and Quantum Computing

Nanotechnology and quantum computing in terms of the hockey stick metaphor are more at the center of the blade with what looks like a number of years or maybe a decade before they create an impact. It is a good idea to keep an eye on each of them, but they are not in the immediate, next three–five year, concern about sudden exponential change. They cannot be dismissed; however, as both private organizations, the military, and nations are pursuing these technologies with interest.

Community colleges can support the research process through periodic report sessions as suggested above. Without formal and informal continual research, the college could find itself left behind when exponential technology changes take place, which could create issues for the college, its students, the business community it serves and local economic development it supports.

Further, it may not be long before colleges will need to employ an administrator in charge of providing formal research and encouraging informal research to keep the college fully informed of potential technological developments that will expand exponentially.

Resetting the Vision

The vision for the college must be developed that includes requiring administrators, faculty, staff and board members to be continually on the lookout for technology changes that might be exponential. Items discussed in this book is a place to begin. Getting everyone in the institution on board formally or informally researching technologies that might affect the college is critical to the institution's future success.

Faculty and Staff Development

As a result of exponentially developing technologies creating new opportunities for the local business community, the college will need to address the training needs for the faculty involved. Constant upgrading of skills of the faculty will be needed to keep up with the changing needs in the workforce.

Unfortunately, this will not be a single event, but will become a constant set of events as the technologies impact the local businesses. The college president and board will need to make certain that sufficient funding is contained in the annual budget of the college to appropriately serve the workforce needs of the business community.

In the past faculty and staff development funding was necessary for the college programs to remain viable. However, in the near future and beyond, development funding will take on a new, critical importance as the business community makes significant, rapid changes due to technological developments. Funding for faculty development will become a high priority in the budget for the college to remain viable for its students and the business community.

Technology and Equipment

Another funding expenditure that will increase is that needed for technology and associated equipment. In order to serve the changing needs of the business community, the latest equipment and technology will be needed at the college.

If the college cannot obtain the required technology and associated equipment, the institution will soon be of little use to the business community or to local economic development. If the state cannot provide the funding for the equipment and technology, it may need to be obtained from alternative sources such as the business community and other alternative means.

Learning to Unlearn

The points made above only delineate what is needed in the *starting blocks* of what is to be a rapid, ever continuing, ever-changing race to stay abreast with what will be needed in the community college arena in the near and far-reaching future. The past is gone. The future will need to be continuously addressed. As the community college movement continues to serve students, the local business community, and economic development, it will repeatedly find new areas through its research that need to be addressed.

Nanotechnology alone could completely modify the way products are developed and manufactured. It could have phenomenal effects in the medical world as well. Bitcoin/Blockchain could turn the current banking system on its head and perhaps replace the current financial accounting practices.

Quantum computing could totally revise everything we know about computers and their effects in the local, regional, national, and international arenas. These three items alone, although still on the periphery, could increase on a Moore's Law exponential curve or much faster with quantum computing. All three would have immense impacts on our society, culture, and community colleges.

Staying the Course

Given the possibilities created by exponential technology change, it may be easy for community college leaders to throw up their hands and resign from the stress of leading an institution. On the other hand, those who choose to successfully lead will refuse to give up and will find ways or make them to keep up with the increasing velocity of change. In addition, the leaders will need to optimistically believe in the future.

CONCLUSION

To some, the future may look frightening with its exponential changes in technology. It will take strong, informed, research minded, rapid acting, caring leaders to understand what is needed, find ways to provide what is needed, and carry on no matter how confusing the situation may appear. The task is not impossible, but it will require innovative and creative methods to successfully handle what is coming.

Community college leaders will have to accept the fact discussed by the Greeks that the only absolute in the universe is change. However, as far as is known, the Greeks did not experience or deal with exponential change. Community college leaders, faculty, staff, board members, and students will have to proceed down that path together, helping each other as much as is humanly possible.

REFERENCE

Uldrich, J. (2007). *Jump the curve: 50 essential strategies to help your company stay ahead of emerging technologies.* Avon, MA: The Platinum Press.

Appendix

The research in the previous chapters uncovered the possible effects each technological development might have on community colleges and what they might do to keep the institution viable and successful. To deal with effects, here are some programs community colleges may need to consider in the future.

Artificial Intelligence

- Cybersecurity
- Cloud Infrastructure
- AI Engineering
- AI Across the Curriculum
- Public Security

Personal Robots

- Personal Robot Training
- Robotics Repair and Maintenance
- Robotic Operator
- Robotic Empathy Software Training

3D Printing

- 3D Printing for Anthropology
- 3D Printing for Biological Sciences
- 3D Printing for Chemistry
- 3D Printing for Machine Tool
- 3D Printing for Welding

Autonomous Vehicles and Drones

- Autonomous Vehicle Fleet Management
- Autonomous Vehicle Maintenance and Repair
- Autonomous Vehicle Systems Technology
- Autonomous Agricultural Systems Technology
- Autonomous Heavy Equipment Maintenance and Repair
- Drone Piloting
- Drone Engineering
- Unmanned Aerial Systems Technology
- Unmanned Drone Pilot Flight Training
- Federal Aviation Administration Drone Certification
- Drone Geographic Information Systems and Mapping
- Drone Photography and Videography Certificate
- Drone Maintenance Diploma
- Law Enforcement Tactical Operations Certificate

The Internet of Things

- Sensor Maintenance and Repair
- Businesses not yet developed

Genome Development: Medical

- Bioinformatics and Tissue Culture
- Genetic Therapy

Genome Development: Agricultural

- Agrigenomics courses
- Agrigenomic programs

Bitcoin and Blockchain

- Bitcoin-Blockchain across the business curricula
- Short courses in Bitcoin-Blockchain

Quantum Computing

- Associate Degree in Quantum Computing
- Short courses in Quantum Computing

About the Contributors

Shakitha Barner holds a master's in math education and an EdS in community college administration. She is currently department chair of transitional studies at Aiken Technical College in Graniteville, South Carolina.

Eva Baucom holds a master's in professional student counseling and an EdS in community college administration. She is currently admissions counselor for the School of Pharmacy at Wingate University in Wingate, North Carolina.

Charlotte Blackwell holds a master's in nursing and an EdS in community college administration. She is currently associate dean at Wake Technical Community College in Raleigh, North Carolina.

Amy Davis holds a master's in adult education, an EdS in higher education, and an EdS in community college administration. She is currently dean of student success at Cleveland Community College in Shelby, North Carolina.

Takeem L. Dean holds a master's in educational leadership: adult and organizational leadership and an EdS in community college administration. He is currently dean of student services at Johnson C. Smith University in Charlotte, North Carolina.

Anthony Dozier holds a master's in educational leadership and an EdS in community college administration. He is currently senior program manager at Wells Fargo in Charlotte, North Carolina.

Travis Gleaton holds a master's in educational leadership and an EdS in community college administration. He is currently associate dean of students at Greenville Technical College in Greenville, South Carolina.

Lonnie F. Griffin III holds a master's in sociology and an EdS in community college administration. He is currently dean of general studies and learning support at Savannah Technical College in Savannah, Georgia.

Cristy Holmes holds a master's in Spanish and Latin American literature and an EdS in community college administration. She is currently department head of academic success at Alamance Community College in Graham, North Carolina.

Melodie Hunnicutt holds a master's in secondary education and an EdS in community college administration. She is currently an adjunct faculty member in social and behavioral sciences at Midlands Technical College in Columbia, South Carolina.

Renie Johnston holds a master's in biology education and an EdS in community college administration. She is currently a faculty member in the biology department at Fayetteville Technical Community College in Fayetteville, North Carolina.

Carlos McCormick holds a master's in educational technology and an EdS in community college administration. He is currently director of media production and learning support services at Wake Technical Community College in Raleigh, North Carolina.

Jaime McLeod holds a master's in instructional technology and an EdS in community college administration. He is currently an instructional designer at Sandhills Community College in Pinehurst, North Carolina.

William "Ben" Shirley holds a master's in sociology and an EdS in community college administration. He is currently a faculty member in the sociology department and honors program coordinator at Alamance Community College in Graham, North Carolina.

John "Scott" Stauble Jr. holds a master's in secondary science education and an EdS in community college administration. He is currently science coordinator at Durham Technical Community College in Durham, North Carolina.

Carolyn Walker holds a master's in career and technical education and an EdS in community college administration. She is currently an office technology faculty member at Greenville Technical College in Greenville, South Carolina.

Natalie Winfree holds a master's in psychology and an EdS in community college administration. She is currently director of counseling services at Montgomery Community College in Troy, North Carolina.

About the Editor

Darrel W. Staat hails from Michigan, where he received a doctorate in English from the University of Michigan, a master's in English from Western Michigan University, and a bachelor's degree in English from Hope College, located in Holland, Michigan.

Since 2015 he has held the position of coordinator and assistant professor of the Community College Executive Leadership Program (CCEL) at Wingate University Ballantyne in Charlotte, North Carolina. He teaches six graduate courses and administers the CCEL program. In 2014, he taught online courses at the undergraduate and graduate levels.

In October 2013, Darrel retired from the position of president of South Carolina Technical College System in Columbia, South Carolina, a position he held for over three years. Previously, he served as president of Central Virginia Community College in Lynchburg, Virginia, for eleven years.

Before that, he served for five years as founding president of York County Community College in Wells, Maine, and four years as president of Eastern Maine Community College in Bangor, Maine. While president of those various institutions, he was highly involved in local economic development and community affairs serving in leadership positions on a considerable number of local boards.

As a faculty member, he spent four years at Southwestern Michigan College in Dowagiac, Michigan. As an administrator, he spent four years at Northeastern Technical College in Cheraw, South Carolina, and thirteen years at Florence–Darlington Technical College in South Carolina. He also taught courses at Coker College, Francis Marion University, and Limestone College, all in South Carolina.

73540109R00083

Made in the USA
Columbia, SC
06 September 2019